THE ATONEMENT

THE
ATONEMENT

FULFILLING GOD'S GREAT
PLAN OF HAPPINESS

EARL C. TINGEY

DESERET
BOOK®

Library of Congress Cataloging-in-Publication Data

Tingey, Earl C. (Earl Carr), 1934–
  The Atonement : fulfilling God's great plan of happiness / Earl C. Tingey.
    p.   cm
  Includes bibliographical references and index.
  ISBN 1-57345-566-0
  1. Atonement.   2. Church of Jesus Christ of Latter-day Saints—Doctrines.   I. Title.
  BX8643.A85T56   2000
  232'.3—dc21

00-031588

Printed in the United States of America   72082-6503
10 9   8   7   6   5   4   3   2

*To my wife, Joanne, our four children and their spouses,
our grandchildren, and a large and noble extended family.
Their faith and example aided in the inspiration
that led to the writing of this book.*

CONTENTS

PREFACE

✳The Atonement of Jesus Christ is the most important event that has ever occurred in the history of the world. Every member of The Church of Jesus Christ of Latter-day Saints should clearly understand the Atonement and live to enjoy the blessings of the Atonement that accrue to the faithful.

Several years ago, in a training meeting for members of the Quorums of the Seventy, we were discussing the Atonement and its relationship to the plan of redemption. As members of the Quorum of the Twelve instructed the Seventy, many of us developed a fuller understanding of the wonderful and beautiful principles of the gospel.

We become aware of sacred truth by studying, praying, and pondering. Those who are lifelong members of the Church add to their knowledge and testimony of the gospel a step and a measure at a time. Converts, on the other hand, may discover gospel truths as soon as they separate their lives from the ways of the world. Whether an understanding and testimony of gospel truths come slowly and quietly or quickly and conspicuously, they come nonetheless to the faithful who study, pray, and ponder.

As members of the Seventy were being taught about the Atonement, we each received an assignment to study the Atonement over the next several months and then prepare a one-page summary of our understanding of the Atonement. This one-page document was to be returned to the Twelve.

I accepted the assignment and commenced the task. Initially, I studied all the scriptures listed in the index and Topical Guide in the LDS edition of the King James version of the Bible under the heading "Jesus Christ, Atonement through" and under related headings. I read and studied each scripture under these headings as well as numerous scripture cross-references.

My study of this wonderful subject became almost an obsession. I devoted many free moments to the assignment. I pursued the study for hours while traveling by air and waiting in airports. I focused personal study each day on acquiring a greater understanding of the Atonement.

I quickly discovered that the more I studied the Atonement, the more there was to study. As my knowledge and understanding grew, I realized that fully comprehending the Atonement was an assignment almost beyond my ability to accomplish in this life.

I soon discovered that there were many writings, conference talks, and articles on the Atonement. Each talk and article further opened my understanding of the Atonement. The material I gathered soon filled many binders. How could all of this understanding of the Atonement be consolidated into one page? It seemed an impossible task.

Finally, after several months of study, I commenced to write the one-page summary of my understanding of the Atonement. It became one of the most difficult undertakings I had ever pursued.

By far, it exceeded my writing and drafting assignments at the university and in professional studies and practice. I had to choose each word carefully so as not to exceed my one-page limit. When I finished, I turned in the paper as requested.

Since then, as I have increased my understanding of the Atonement, I have rewritten my original paper to reflect my extended knowledge and grasp. I will continue to rewrite my understanding of the Atonement as I continue to discover and study additional books and articles.

The magnitude of materials available on this topic became obvious during my studies. How could I ever comprehend all the materials clearly and simply? That question led to this book; yet only a small portion of all I collected and studied is contained here.

Gifted Church leaders have written much about the Atonement in more philosophical terms. My approach in this book has been to focus on elementary and basic scriptures and writings on the Atonement. This book is meant as a tool for new members of the Church and for others who may just be initiating their study of the Atonement. I have attempted to include all the very basic and essential teachings that give understanding of the Atonement.

Every member of the Church and every honest and faithful person studying the gospel is entitled to know the basic and essential doctrines that explain the Atonement. No one could presume to include in one book all that is basic and essential to the Atonement, but this book contains many of those doctrines.

Understanding the importance and origin of the Atonement is necessary in order to gain a testimony of the Atonement. The scriptures are clear, unequivocal, and consistent in this respect.

The personal discovery of the relationship of the Atonement of Jesus Christ to the law of Moses was a marvelous awakening for me.

An understanding of this truth would bless the people of the world who do not yet accept the Savior.

The singular importance of the Book of Mormon in revealing and preserving many precious truths of the Atonement became evident as I proceeded with my study. Discovering that these New World people so clearly understood much of the mission of Jesus Christ before he was born on earth became a personal revelation to me.

The clear writings in the Book of Mormon concerning the Creation and the Fall and the conditions that prevailed in the Garden of Eden are necessary to understanding the Atonement. The clarity of the Book of Mormon in describing the mission of Jesus Christ and his personal attributes that made the Atonement possible contributes to a more clear understanding of biblical scriptures.

Latter-day Saints enter into ordinances, including ordinances in holy temples, as they take upon themselves sacred covenants to keep the commandments of God. All of this is a part of becoming eligible for the full and complete blessings of the Atonement. Knowing how this religious practice applies to the Atonement is basic and essential.

Understanding the Atonement includes knowledge of how it applies to those who have died without law and without knowledge of Jesus Christ. What happens to little children who die before baptism or to those born with diminished mental capacity? How does the Atonement affect their lives?

Fortunately, the teachings of latter-day prophets sustain the scriptures and the writings of former-day prophets. These watchmen help us understand what the Atonement is and how we can live a life that will qualify us to become eligible for its full blessings.

It is expected that as you study this book, you will gain a more clear and comprehensive understanding of the Atonement. Perhaps you might attempt to summarize in one page your understanding of

My Challenge

the Atonement. Over the years I have invited hundreds of full-time missionaries to study the doctrine of the Atonement and express their understanding in one page. Many of these simple statements from humble missionaries are as comprehensive and understandable as the many writings studied in preparation of this book.

As you study and apply the doctrines of the Atonement in your everyday life, you will gain personal assurances pertaining to the mission of Jesus Christ. It is my hope that you will come to know that Jesus is the Christ, that he wrought the Atonement for our benefit, and that we are eternally indebted to him.

ACKNOWLEDGMENTS

I extend thanks and gratitude to Michael Morris and others who professionally and skillfully assisted in the editing. I also express my appreciation to Pat Fought and to my secretary, Bonnie Phelps, for their patience, careful attention to detail, and typing of the manuscript. In addition, I wish to acknowledge the encouragement of Ronald Millett, Sheri Dew, and Cory Maxwell.

I
THE IMPORTANCE OF THE ATONEMENT

The third article of faith states: "We believe that through the Atonement of Christ, all mankind may be saved, by obedience to the laws and ordinances of the Gospel." This article does not say that all mankind will be saved; it says that all mankind may be saved. The principle of choice is preserved for every person.

Lehi taught the same doctrine: "Adam fell that men might be; and men are, that they might have joy. And the Messiah cometh in the fulness of time, that he may redeem the children of men from the fall. And because that they are redeemed from the fall they have become free forever, knowing good from evil; to act for themselves and not to be acted upon, . . .

"Wherefore, men are free . . . to choose liberty and eternal life, through the great Mediator of all men, or to choose captivity and death, according to the captivity and power of the devil" (2 Nephi 2:25–27; emphasis added).

The salvation spoken of in the third article of faith and by Lehi is "eternal life"—a conditional salvation in the kingdom of God as distinguished from the Resurrection only.

PHYSICAL AND SPIRITUAL DEATH

The Atonement of Jesus Christ consists of the means by which the two deaths, physical death and spiritual death, can be overcome: "And because of the way of deliverance of our God, the Holy One of Israel, this death, of which I have spoken, which is the temporal, shall deliver up its dead; which death is the grave.

"And this death of which I have spoken, which is the spiritual death, shall deliver up its dead; which spiritual death is hell; wherefore, death and hell must deliver up their dead, and hell must deliver up its captive spirits, and the grave must deliver up its captive bodies, and the bodies and the spirits of men will be restored one to the other; and it is by the power of the resurrection of the Holy One of Israel" (2 Nephi 9:11–12).

Temporal death means a "temporary" separation of the body and the spirit. This is the death we see and mourn. Spiritual death is the separation of the spirit from God forever. We are temporally separated from God the Father by being born on this earth. To be forever separated from him following our death and resurrection because we did not live a clean and pure life is the greatest of all tragedies. Repentance, which provides that we may be cleansed from sin and freed from the bondage of transgression, is available to all who constantly strive to overcome spiritual death.

The Resurrection is universal and comes as a gift to all mankind. But to be resurrected is not to enjoy the blessing of eternal life. That blessing, which includes the privilege of living in the presence of the Father and the Son as families, is available only to those who obey the laws and comply with the ordinances of the gospel.

THE PLAN'S IMPORTANCE

It is important to know that God has prepared a plan whereby his children might return to live with him. The Atonement is a critical element of that plan. The Book of Mormon prophet Jacob said of this plan:

"O the wisdom of God, his mercy and grace! For behold, if the flesh should rise no more our spirits must become subject to that angel who fell from before the presence of the Eternal God, and became the devil, to rise no more.

"And our spirits must have become like unto him, and we become devils, angels to a devil, to be shut out from the presence of our God, and to remain with the father of lies, in misery, like unto himself; yea, to that being who beguiled our first parents, who transformeth himself nigh unto an angel of light, and stirreth up the children of men unto secret combinations of murder and all manner of secret works of darkness.

"O how great the goodness of our God, who prepareth a way for our escape from the grasp of this awful monster; yea, that monster, death and hell, which I call the death of the body, and also the death of the spirit" (2 Nephi 9:8–10).

Elder Bruce R. McConkie spoke of the Atonement and its essential role in mankind's effort to receive salvation under the plan of redemption: "The Atonement is the most transcendent doctrine of the Gospel. It is the most important single thing that has ever occurred in the history of the world, or ever will occur. It is the foundation upon which all other things rest. If it weren't for the Atonement, we could write the Gospel off as a myth and the whole purpose of the creation would be frustrated."[1]

Having an unshakeable knowledge and testimony of the Atonement ought to be the quest and desire of every God-fearing person. Jacob said, "And now, beloved, marvel not that I tell you

3

these things; for why not speak of the atonement of Christ, and attain to a perfect knowledge of him, as to attain to the knowledge of a resurrection and the world to come?" (Jacob 4:12).

THE ROLE OF MANKIND

To more fully understand the Atonement and its divine role in fulfilling the plan of redemption established by God and fully implemented by his loving and obedient Son, Jesus Christ, we must appreciate our role in the plan. In a marvelous and insightful book written in 1882, President John Taylor, third president of the Church, discussed the role and limitations of mankind.

"Man, as man, can only make use of the powers which are possessed by man. Made, indeed, as represented in the Scriptures, in the image of God, as monarch of the universe he stands erect on the earth in the likeness of his Great Creator; beautifully constructed in all his parts, with a body possessing all the functions necessary for the wants of humanity; standing, not only by right, but by adaptability, beauty, symmetry and glory, at the head of all creation; . . . and the representative of God upon the earth. But while he occupies this exalted position, and is in the image of God, yet he possesses simply, as a man, only the powers which belong to man; and is subject to weakness, infirmity, disease and death. And when he dies, without some superior aid pertaining to the future, that noble structure lies silent and helpless, its organs, that heretofore were active, lively and energetic, are now dormant, inactive and powerless. And what of the mind, that before went back into eternity and reached forward into eternity? And what of its powers? Or what of that spirit, which, with its Godlike energies, its prescience and power, could grasp infinity? What of it, and where is it? The Scriptures say that the body returns to the dust and the spirit returns to God who gave it. But what of its powers as made known to us, what of the hereafter? The philosophy of the world tells us that the spirit dies with the body, and like it is dissipated in surrounding nature, but as an entirety no longer exists; and all the power the being ever had was to propagate its own species and to impart the powers of the body and the mind to its posterity. Such philosophers can comprehend nothing pertaining to the future—no glory, no exaltation, no eternal progression, only as developed by a succession of manhood. If, then, there is a spirit in man which reaches into futurity, that would grasp eternal progress, eternal enjoyments, and eternal exaltations; then those glories, those exaltations, those capabilities and those powers must be the gift of some superior being, power, or authority to that which exists in man; for the foregoing is a brief exhibition of the powers and capabilities of humanity. It is of this gift that we now speak. It is of a principle that emanates from God, that originates with a superior intelligence, whose plans, and powers, and capabilities are exalted above those of mortal man, as the heavens are above the earth, or as the majestic works of the Great Creator throughout the infinitude of space are superior to the puny efforts of the children of mortality. It is for the exaltation of man to this state of superior intelligence and Godhead that the mediation and Atonement of Jesus Christ is instituted; and that noble being, man, made in the image of God, is rendered capable not only of being a son of man, but also a son of God, through adoption, and is rendered capable of becoming a God, possessing the power, the majesty, the exaltation and the position of a God. . . .

"This transition from his manhood to the Godhead can alone be made through a power which is superior to man—an infinite power, an eternal power, even the power of the Godhead: for as in Adam all die, so in Christ *only* can all be made alive" (1 Corinthians 15:22).[2]

UNDERSTANDING THE COMMANDMENTS AND THE PLAN

In attempting to teach the gospel to Zeezrom, the misguided but later repentant and baptized lawyer, Alma put the need to understand the Atonement into perspective in the following verse: "Therefore God gave unto them commandments, *after* having made known unto them the plan of redemption, that they should not do evil, the penalty thereof being a second death, which was an everlasting death as to things pertaining unto righteousness; for on such the plan of redemption could have no power, for the works of justice could not be destroyed, according to the supreme goodness of God" (Alma 12:32; emphasis added).

The key word in this passage is *after*. An understanding of the commandments—the "divine directives for righteous living" that "bring happiness and spiritual and temporal blessings"³—should be preceded by an understanding of the plan of redemption, which includes the Atonement. So often we teach, tell, and require others to keep certain rules and commandments without their fully understanding why.

Knowing the fulness of the plan of redemption gives purpose and meaning to trying to keep the commandments. Why be morally clean? Why perform service? Why be a good neighbor? Why repent and be baptized? Why enter the temple, make sacred covenants, and strive to keep them all the days of your life?

Why? Because by exercising our moral agency righteously, we live lives that will permit us to return to live forever with our Heavenly Father and his Son. That opportunity and promised reward should be an overriding goal, desire, and motivation in all that we do.

It is more difficult to keep a commandment solely because we are told to do so than because we believe it is the right thing to do.

It is easier to keep a commandment when we know that keeping it leads to the privilege of enjoying eternal life.

JOYFUL EXPRESSIONS OF THE ATONEMENT

The Atonement is a vital part of the great and eternal plan of redemption. Jacob spoke of the Atonement in joyful expressions of thanksgiving: "O the wisdom of God, his mercy and grace!" "O how great the goodness of our God." "O how great the plan of our God!" "O the greatness and the justice of our God!" "O the greatness of the mercy of our God. . . !" "O how great the holiness of our God!" (2 Nephi 9:8, 10, 13, 17, 19, 20).

Jacob's joyful expressions came from gratitude for knowing what would occur but for the Atonement: "Our spirits must have become like unto him, and we become devils, angels to a devil, to be shut out from the presence of our God, and to remain with the father of lies, in misery, like unto himself" (2 Nephi 9:9).

Because of Christ's Atonement, a way has been prepared "for our escape from the grasp of this awful monster; yea, that monster, death [physical death] and hell [spiritual death], which I call the death of the body, and also the death of the spirit. . . .

". . . For he delivereth his saints from that awful monster the devil, and death, and hell, and that lake of fire and brimstone, which is endless torment. . . . And if they will not repent and believe in his name, and be baptized in his name, and endure to the end, they must be damned" (2 Nephi 9:10, 19, 24).

In a moment of marvelous testimony in which Nephi declared that he and Jacob had seen the Redeemer (2 Nephi 11:2–3), Nephi said, "And my soul delighteth in proving unto my people that save Christ should come all men must perish" (2 Nephi 11:6).

Amulek defined the importance of the Atonement as a necessary part of the plan of salvation by declaring that it is "the great plan of the Eternal God" and that without an Atonement, "all mankind must unavoidably perish; yea, all are hardened; yea, all are fallen and are lost, and must perish except it be through the atonement which it is expedient should be made" (Alma 34:9).

Alma, in teaching his wayward son Corianton, referred to the plan of redemption as "the great plan of happiness": "Now behold, it was not expedient that man should be reclaimed from this temporal death [the fall in the Garden of Eden], for that would destroy the *great plan of happiness*" (Alma 42:8; emphasis added).

If we appreciate that our choices can provide us with an opportunity to live eternally with our Heavenly Father, we are on our way to understanding the Atonement. This life can truly become the pursuit of eternal happiness.

THE ATONEMENT IS THE MOST VITAL PART OF THE GREAT PLAN OF HAPPINESS

It is God's plan to reward us eternal happiness with him and his Son if we, by proper use of our agency, willingly obey the commandments and endure to the end. And so, when we speak of the Atonement, we speak of the voluntary act of Jesus Christ, the Only Begotten Son of God, who came to earth to provide a means whereby all mankind could elect to return to their loving Father. This "great plan of happiness" is important to us and should inspire us to qualify under the provisions of the Atonement to receive salvation and eternal life.

"Ye are free to act for yourselves—to choose the way of everlasting death or the way of eternal life. Wherefore, my beloved brethren, reconcile yourselves to the will of God, and not to the will of the devil and the flesh; and remember, after ye are reconciled unto God, that it is only in and though the grace of God that ye are saved.

"Wherefore, may God raise you from death by the power of the resurrection, and also from everlasting death by the power of the atonement, that ye may be received into the eternal kingdom of God, that ye may praise him through grace divine. Amen" (2 Nephi 10:23–25).

NOTES

1. Bruce R. McConkie, *The Atonement*, Brigham Young University Speaches of the Year (Provo, Utah: 6 May 1953), 1.

2. John Taylor, *The Mediation and Atonement* (Salt Lake City: Deseret News, 1882), 139–41.

3. "Commandments," *Encyclopedia of Mormonism*, ed. Daniel H. Ludlow, 4 vols. (New York: Macmillan Publishing, 1992), 1:296.

II
PREPARED FROM THE
FOUNDATION OF THE WORLD

What is known or revealed about the origin of the great plan of happiness? Did knowledge of that plan originate at the birth of Jesus Christ or was it made known earlier? Did Adam and Eve know of the plan? How much has God revealed about the marvelous plan whereby the Atonement can become effective in the lives of his children?

THE ORIGIN OF THE GREAT PLAN OF HAPPINESS

Fortunately, a loving Heavenly Father has provided through revelation to ancient and modern prophets all of the knowledge and information necessary for mankind to receive salvation and gain eternal life. For Latter-day Saints, additional scriptures found in the Book of Mormon, the Pearl of Great Price, and the Doctrine and Covenants provide added testimony and witness of the origin of the plan of salvation and the Atonement. As we explore, study, and ponder these additional scriptures, as well as the Bible, and as we read statements by latter-day prophets, we will more fully comprehend how much our Father in Heaven loves us and how indebted we are to his Son, Jesus Christ, our Lord and Redeemer, who voluntarily accepted his role in providing the Atonement for each of us.

Let us now begin to discover some of the truths contained in the wonderful and remarkable revelations that testify of the plan of salvation and the Atonement. Revelations teach us that the Atonement transcends all mortal timetables. It existed before Adam and Eve were placed on the earth, originating in the pre-earth life. It was explained at the Grand Council in heaven.

Speaking to the Brigham Young University student body, President Joseph Fielding Smith of the Quorum of the Twelve Apostles said the Atonement of Jesus Christ is the biggest and most vital thing in the world:

"It is vital to every soul born into this world, for every soul born into this world receives the benefit of it. In order to understand the reason for the Atonement, we must go back to the beginning. We are taught in our scriptures that we are the sons and daughters of God, that He is literally our Father, the Father of our spirits, that we dwelt in His presence, and that we have seen Him. There is not a soul here that has not seen Him and who did not dwell in His presence, and when we came into this world all our former knowledge and understanding was taken away and for a wise purpose was erased. But there in that spirit world we had not reached, nor could we reach, the end of our existence, that is, the ultimate reward. It was essential that the opportunity be given to us, to come to this earth where we could receive bodies of flesh and bones, tabernacles for our spirits."[1]

Elder Bruce R. McConkie taught that the Atonement was part of the divine plan: "When this plan, this gospel of God, was presented by the Father to all his spirit children in the councils of eternity, the need for a Savior and Redeemer was set forth in full. After the doctrine of the fall and the plan of redemption had been set forth in all their wonder and glory, the Father sent forth a great proclamation to this effect: 'Whom shall I send to be my Son; who will be the Only Begotten in the flesh; who of all my spirit sons shall dwell among mortals with the divine power to atone for their sins; who will go down as the Savior and Redeemer?' (Abraham 3:27–28; Moses 4:1–4.)

"The choice fell upon the Firstborn. He who was beloved and chosen from the beginning then became the Lamb slain from the foundation of the world; he was then chosen and foreordained to be the One who would work out the infinite and eternal atonement. 'Behold, I am he who was prepared from the foundation of the world to redeem my people,' he said to the brother of Jared. 'Behold, I am Jesus Christ.' (Ether 3:14.) And so before mortal men were, before Adam fell that men might be, before there was mortality and procreation and death—before all this, provision was made for the redemption. Then it was decreed that 'the Lord Omnipotent who reigneth, who was, and is from all eternity to all eternity,' should go 'down from heaven among the children of men, and . . . dwell in a tabernacle of clay.'"[2]

THE ATONEMENT WAS KNOWN FROM THE BEGINNING

In his dialogue with Zeezrom, Alma taught and testified of the premortal plan for the Atonement: "Now, if it had not been for the plan of redemption, *which was laid from the foundation of the world*, there could have been no resurrection of the dead; but there was a plan of redemption laid, which shall bring to pass the resurrection of the dead, of which has been spoken" (Alma 12:25; emphasis added).

Alma then explained that what took place in the Garden of Eden was anticipated by the foreordained plan: "And now behold, if it were possible that our first parents could have gone forth and partaken of the tree of life they would have been forever miserable, having no preparatory state; and thus the plan of redemption would have been frustrated, and the word of God would have been void, taking none effect.

"But behold, it was not so; but it was appointed unto men that they must die; and after death, they must come to judgment, even that same judgment of which we have spoken, which is the end. And after God had appointed that these things should come unto man, behold, then he saw that it was expedient that man should know concerning the things whereof he had appointed unto them" (Alma 12:26–28).

The plan of redemption—prepared by a wise, loving Father in Heaven in the pre-earth life—provides a means whereby the Father's children can leave his presence, walk by faith, righteously exercise their agency, and return to his presence. This plan was set forth and explained to all of us in the pre-earth life. We were there, and we learned of the plan.

We no longer remember the plan because a veil has been drawn over our eyes, but the prophets and scriptures testify of that great and marvelous event. Of the events in the Garden of Eden, Alma also said: "And they began from that time forth to call on his name; therefore God conversed with men, and made known unto them the plan of redemption, *which had been prepared from the foundation of the world*; and this he made known unto them according to their faith and repentance and their holy works" (Alma 12:30; emphasis added).

The testimony of every prophet, both ancient and modern, bears witness that the great plan of happiness—which includes the plan of redemption and the Atonement—is eternal and was prepared from the foundation of the world. As Alma testified, prophets are divinely taught and therefore know and teach those truths: "Therefore he sent angels to converse with them, who caused men to behold of his glory" (Alma 12:29).

Hugh Nibley reaffirmed, through reference to secular history, that the Atonement was revealed and established in the Grand Council of Heaven: "What is it in the religion revealed to Joseph Smith that is so different from the others that sound so much like it? The difference is the literal Atonement. The point that places the gospel of Jesus Christ worlds apart from the ideas of others is the concept of sin. . . .

"Joseph Smith took the gospel of Christ back even before Abraham to Adam and beyond, revealing the Atonement as 'the plan of redemption . . . prepared from the foundation of the world' (Alma 12:30). . . .

". . . There is not a word among those translated as 'atonement' which does not plainly indicate the return to a former state or condition; one rejoins the family, returns to the Father, becomes united, reconciled, embracing and sitting down happily with others after a sad separation."[3]

John the Revelator spoke of the War in Heaven and of Christ's victory over Satan: "And there was war in heaven: Michael and his angels fought against the dragon; and the dragon fought and his angels, And prevailed not; neither was their place found any more in heaven. And the great dragon was cast out, that old serpent, called the Devil, and Satan, which deceiveth the whole world: he was cast out into the earth, and his angels were cast out with him.

"And I heard a loud voice saying in heaven, Now is come salvation, and strength, and the kingdom of our God, and the power of his Christ: for the accuser of our brethren is cast down, which accused them before our God day and night. And they overcame him by the blood of the Lamb, and by the word of their testimony; and they loved not their lives unto the death.

"Therefore rejoice, ye heavens, and ye that dwell in them. Woe to the inhabiters of the earth and of the sea! for the devil is come down unto you, having great wrath, because he knoweth that he hath but a short time" (Revelation 12:7–12).

The "blood of the lamb" is the blood that Christ shed through the Atonement. Other prophets have also testified of the Atonement.

Nephi testified that all things from the beginning of the world prove the truth of the coming of Christ: "Behold, my soul delighteth in proving unto my people the truth of the coming of Christ; for, for this end hath the law of Moses been given; and all things which have been given of God from the beginning of the world, unto man, are the typifying of him" (2 Nephi 11:4).

Jacob taught Sherem: "It has been made manifest unto me, for I have heard and seen; and it also has been made manifest unto me by the power of the Holy Ghost; wherefore, I know if there should be no atonement made all mankind must be lost" (Jacob 7:12).

Amulek testified that without the "great plan of the Eternal God" all is lost. He confirmed the premortal existence of the plan: "And now, behold, I will testify unto you of myself that these things are true. Behold, I say unto you, that I do know that Christ shall come among the children of men, to take upon him the transgressions of his people, and that he shall atone for the sins of the world; for the Lord God hath spoken it.

"For it is expedient that an atonement should be made; for according to the great plan of the Eternal God there must be an atonement made, or else all mankind must unavoidably perish; yea, all are hardened; yea, all are fallen and are lost, and must perish except it be through the atonement which it is expedient should be made" (Alma 34:8–9).

King Benjamin taught the Nephites of the coming of Christ and testified that holy prophets had always declared the mission of Christ: "And the Lord God hath sent his holy prophets among all the children of men, to declare these things to every kindred, nation, and tongue, that thereby whosoever should believe that Christ should come, the same might receive remission of their sins, and rejoice with exceedingly great joy, even as though he had already come among them" (Mosiah 3:13).

King Benjamin further instructed the people that the Atonement had been prepared from the foundation of the world: "I say unto you, if ye have come to a knowledge of the goodness of God, and his matchless power, and his wisdom, and his patience, and his long-suffering towards the children of men; and also, *the atonement which has been prepared from the foundation of the world,* that thereby salvation might come to him that should put his trust in the Lord, and should be diligent in keeping his commandments, and continue in the faith even unto the end of his life, I mean the life of the mortal body—

"I say, that this is the man who receiveth salvation, through *the atonement which was prepared from the foundation of the world* for all mankind, which ever were since the fall of Adam, or who are, or who ever shall be, even unto the end of the world" (Mosiah 4:6–7; emphasis added).

Enoch was taught that the Atonement took effect from the foundation of the world—hence, original sin is not answered on the head of mankind: "Hence came the saying abroad among the people, that the Son of God hath atoned for original guilt, wherein the sins of the parents cannot be answered upon the heads of the children, for they are whole from the foundation of the world" (Moses 6:54).

Elder Bruce R. McConkie declared: "The doctrine of the atonement embraces, sustains, supports, and gives life and force to all other gospel doctrines."[4]

In a beautiful vision to the Prophet Joseph Smith, the Lord revealed the qualifications of entering the celestial kingdom, explaining the central role of Jesus Christ in establishing the gospel to teach the Atonement: "And this is the gospel, the glad tidings, which the voice out of the heavens bore record unto us—that he came into the world, even Jesus, to be crucified for the world, and to bear the sins of the world, and to sanctify the world, and to cleanse it from all unrighteousness; that through him all might be saved whom the Father had put into his power and made by him" (D&C 76:40–42).

Elder McConkie added: "To the Nephites the resurrected Lord spoke similarly: 'Behold I have given unto you my gospel, and this is the gospel which I have given unto you—that I came into the world to do the will of my Father, because my Father sent me. And my Father sent me that I might be lifted up upon the cross.' (3 Ne. 27:13–14.)

"Salvation comes because of the atonement. Without it the whole plan of salvation would be frustrated and the whole purpose behind the creating and populating of the earth would come to naught. With it the eternal purposes of the Father will roll forth, the purpose of creation be preserved, the plan of salvation made efficacious, and men will be assured of a hope of the highest exaltation hereafter."[5]

NOTES

1. Joseph Fielding Smith, *The Atonement of Jesus Christ*, Brigham Young University Speeches of the Year (Provo, Utah: 25 January 1955), 1.

2. Bruce R. McConkie, *A New Witness for the Articles of Faith* (Salt Lake City: Deseret Book, 1985), 110–11.

3. Hugh Nibley, "The Atonement of Jesus Christ," *Ensign*, August 1990, 33.

4. Bruce R. McConkie, *Mormon Doctrine, 2d ed.* (Salt Lake City: Deseret Book, 1966), 60.

5. McConkie, *Mormon Doctrine*, 60–61.

III
ATONEMENT, SACRIFICE, AND THE LAW OF MOSES

The Atonement was prepared from the foundation of the world but not fully accomplished until Jesus Christ came in the meridian of time. What, then, is the significance of the religious practices of the people who preceded the birth of Christ? Were the world's ancient inhabitants eligible for the blessings attainable through the Atonement? What role do the law of Moses and the early practices of sacrifice from the days of Adam to Jesus Christ play in the Atonement?

The principle of sacrifice was an essential part of the worship and religious life of those who were subject to the law of Moses, but sacrifice preceded the time of Moses and was spoken of during the time of Adam and Eve. To fully understand the Atonement, we must understand the principle of sacrifice and the purpose of the law of Moses.

THE PRINCIPLE OF SACRIFICE

The Lord introduced the principle of sacrifice to Adam and Eve after they were cast out of the Garden of Eden: "And he gave unto them commandments, that they should worship the Lord their God, and should offer the firstlings of their flocks, for an offering unto the Lord. And Adam was obedient unto the commandments of the Lord.

"And after many days an angel of the Lord appeared unto Adam, saying: Why dost thou offer sacrifices unto the Lord? And Adam said unto him: I know not, save the Lord commanded me.

"And then the angel spake, saying: This thing is a similitude of the sacrifice of the Only Begotten of the Father, which is full of grace and truth. Wherefore, thou shalt do all that thou doest in the name of the Son, and thou shalt repent and call upon God in the name of the Son forevermore" (Moses 5:5–8).

"Thus," as Elder McConkie observed, "sacrifice was first instituted on earth as a gospel ordinance to be performed by the authority of the priesthood, to typify the coming sacrifice of the Son of God for the sins of the world. From the day of Adam to the death of Christ, sacrifice was practiced by the saints."[1]

Sacrifice became an essential part of the rites of worship of ancient Israel. The Nephites also offered sacrifices (1 Nephi 5:9; 1 Nephi 7:22). When Abraham was tested, his absolute obedience was tested in the commandment he received to offer a burnt offering to God. Abraham was prepared to offer his only son, Isaac, until he was stayed by an angel of the Lord (Genesis 22:1–13). President John Taylor has written that Abraham offered "sacrifice in token of the great expiatory sacrifice of the Son of God."[2]

The similitude of Abraham's preparedness to sacrifice Isaac points to the sacrifice of Jesus Christ allowed by God the Eternal Father. John the Baptist declared that Christ was "the Lamb of God, which taketh away the sin of the world" (John 1:29). And as he looked upon Jesus, John said, "Behold the Lamb of God!" (John 1:36).

THE SIGNIFICANCE OF THE PASSOVER

The sacrifice of a lamb took on new and special meaning at the time of Moses. The hardness of Pharaoh's heart in refusing to let Moses and the children of Israel leave Egypt resulted in many plagues upon the Egyptians. The last plague, as declared by Moses, was that "the firstborn in the land of Egypt shall die" (Exodus 11:5). To prevent this plague from afflicting the Israelites, the Lord instituted the Passover.

"And the Lord spake unto Moses and Aaron in the land of Egypt, saying, This month shall be unto you the beginning of months: it shall be the first month of the year to you.

"Speak ye unto all the congregation of Israel, saying, In the tenth day of this month they shall take to them every man a lamb, according to the house of their fathers, a lamb for an house: And if the household be too little for the lamb, let him and his neighbour next unto his house take it according to the number of the souls; every man according to his eating shall make your count for the lamb.

"Your lamb shall be without blemish, a male of the first year: ye shall take it out from the sheep, or from the goats: And ye shall keep it up until the fourteenth day of the same month: and the whole assembly of the congregation of Israel shall kill it in the evening.

"And they shall take of the blood, and strike it on the two side posts and on the upper door post of the houses, wherein they shall eat it. And they shall eat the flesh in that night, roast with fire, and unleavened bread; and with bitter herbs they shall eat it. . . . And thus shall ye eat it; with your loins girded, your shoes on your feet, and your staff in your hand; and ye shall eat it in haste: it is the Lord's passover.

"For I will pass through the land of Egypt this night, and will smite all the firstborn in the land of Egypt, both man and beast; and against all the gods of Egypt I will execute judgment: I am the Lord. And the blood shall be to you for a token upon the houses where ye are: and when I see the blood, I will pass over you, and the plague shall not be upon you to destroy you, when I smite the land of Egypt.

"And this day shall be unto you for a memorial; and ye shall keep it a feast to the Lord throughout your generations; ye shall keep it a feast by an ordinance for ever" (Exodus 12:1–14).

Concerning this scripture, Elder Bruce R. McConkie wrote: "The sacrificial offering made in connection with the Passover, the killing of the Paschal Lamb, for instance, was so arranged that a male lamb of the first year, one without spot or blemish, was chosen; in the offering the blood was spilled and care was taken to break no bones—all symbolical of the manner of Christ's death. (Ex. 12.) Many sacrificial details were added to the law as it operated in the Mosaic dispensation, but the basic principles governing sacrifices are part of the gospel itself and preceded Moses and the lesser order which came through him."[3]

President John Taylor provided additional insight: "When the destroying angel passed by the houses of the children of Israel he found the blood of a lamb sprinkled on the door post; which was a type of the blood of Christ, the Lamb of God. The angel who was the executor of justice could not touch those who were protected by that sacred symbol; because that prefigured the sacrifice of the Son of God, which was provided at the beginning of creation for the redemption of the human family, and which was strictly in accordance with provisions then made by the Almighty for that purpose—'the Lamb slain from before the foundation of the world' [Revelation 13:8; Moses 7:47]—and accepted in full as an atonement for the transgressions of mankind, according to the requirements of eternal justice and agreed to by the Savior and His Father."[4]

The Mosaic dispensation included not only the Passover but many additional gospel truths, including the Ten Commandments (Exodus 20) and the opportunity for people to enjoy the blessings of the lesser priesthood, often referred to as the Aaronic or Levitical Priesthood. This law and practice, initiated by Moses, became, in the words of Paul, "our schoolmaster to bring us unto Christ, that we might be justified by faith" (Galatians 3:24).

Modern scripture confirms that the children of Israel under Moses were limited to the blessings of the lesser priesthood: "Now this Moses plainly taught to the children of Israel in the wilderness, and sought diligently to sanctify his people that they might behold the face of God; but they hardened their hearts and could not endure his presence; therefore, the Lord in his wrath, for his anger was kindled against them, swore that they should not enter into his rest while in the wilderness, which rest is the fulness of his glory.

"Therefore, he took Moses out of their midst, and the Holy Priesthood also; and the lesser priesthood continued, which priesthood holdeth the key of the ministering of angels and the preparatory gospel" (D&C 84:23–26).

LAW OF MOSES PREPARED FOR THE MISSION OF JESUS CHRIST

It was not intended that salvation come through the law of Moses but through Christ. Four hundred years before the birth of Christ, Jacob labored mightily to preserve the record of his people and the reasons they worshiped God in the name of Christ. The intimate knowledge of Christ's mission over four hundred years before he was born to Mary is a testimony of the truthfulness of the Book of Mormon.

"Now behold, it came to pass that I, Jacob, having ministered much unto my people in word, (and I cannot write but a little of my words, because of the difficulty of engraving our words upon plates) and we know that the things which we write upon plates must remain;

"But whatsoever things we write upon anything save it be upon plates must perish and vanish away; but we can write a few words upon plates, which will give our children, and also our beloved brethren, a small degree of knowledge concerning us, or concerning their fathers—

"Now in this thing we do rejoice; and we labor diligently to engraven these words upon plates, hoping that our beloved brethren and our children will receive them with thankful hearts, and look upon them that they may learn with joy and not with sorrow, neither with contempt, concerning their first parents.

"For, for this intent have we written these things, that they may know that we knew of Christ, and we had a hope of his glory many hundred years before his coming; and not only we ourselves had a hope of his glory, but also all the holy prophets which were before us.

"Behold, they believed in Christ and worshiped the Father in his name, and also we worship the Father in his name. And for this intent we keep the law of Moses, it pointing our souls to him; and for this cause it is sanctified unto us for righteousness, even as it was accounted unto Abraham in the wilderness to be obedient unto the commands of God in offering up his son Isaac, which is a similitude of God and his Only Begotten Son" (Jacob 4:1–5).

The Nephites understood and kept the law of Moses in recognition of the forthcoming mission of the Lord and Savior, Jesus Christ. Nephi earlier testified that the law of Moses typified Christ and proved that he would come: "Behold, my soul delighteth in proving unto my people the truth of the coming of Christ; for, for this end hath the law of Moses been given; and all things which have been given of God from the beginning of the world, unto man, are the typifying of him.

"And also my soul delighteth in the covenants of the Lord which he hath made to our fathers; yea, my soul delighteth in his grace, and in his justice, and power, and mercy in the great and eternal plan of deliverance from death.

"And my soul delighteth in proving unto my people that save Christ should come all men must perish. For if there be no Christ there be no God; and if there be no God we are not, for there could have been no creation. But there is a God, and he is Christ, and he cometh in the fulness of his own time" (2 Nephi 11:4–7).

King Benjamin taught the purpose of the law of Moses: "Yet the Lord God saw that his people were a stiffnecked people, and he appointed unto them a law, even the law of Moses. And many signs, and wonders, and types, and shadows showed he unto them, concerning his coming; and also holy prophets spake unto them concerning his coming; and yet they hardened their hearts, and understood not that the law of Moses availeth nothing except it were through the atonement of his blood" (Mosiah 3:14–15).

TYPES AND SHADOWS OF THINGS TO COME

The "types and shadows" of the coming of Christ required great faith of those who lived before the meridian of time. Moroni wrote, "Wherefore, by faith was the law of Moses given" (Ether 12:11). By looking back on history we see more perfectly a pattern and purpose for the law of Moses, and we can more completely understand that "the law of Moses availeth nothing except it were through the atonement of [Christ's] blood" (Mosiah 3:15).

Twenty-five years after King Benjamin spoke of the law of

Moses, Abinadi taught similar doctrine, referring to the law of Moses as "types of things to come": "And now ye have said that salvation cometh by the law of Moses. I say unto you that it is expedient that ye should keep the law of Moses as yet; but I say unto you, that the time shall come when it shall no more be expedient to keep the law of Moses.

"And moreover, I say unto you, that salvation doth not come by the law alone; and were it not for the atonement, which God himself shall make for the sins and iniquities of his people, that they must unavoidably perish, notwithstanding the law of Moses.

"And now I say unto you that it was expedient that there should be a law given to the children of Israel, yea, even a very strict law; for they were a stiffnecked people, quick to do iniquity, and slow to remember the Lord their God; therefore there was a law given them, yea, a law of performances and of ordinances, a law which they were to observe strictly from day to day, to keep them in remembrance of God and their duty towards him. But behold, I say unto you, that all these things were types of things to come.

"And now, did they understand the law? I say unto you, Nay, they did not all understand the law; and this because of the hardness of their hearts; for they understood not that there could not any man be saved except it were through the redemption of God. For behold, did not Moses prophesy unto them concerning the coming of the Messiah, and that God should redeem his people? Yea, and even all the prophets who have prophesied ever since the world began—have they not spoken more or less concerning these things?

"Have they not said that God himself should come down among the children of men, and take upon him the form of man, and go forth in mighty power upon the face of the earth? Yea, and have they not said also that he should bring to pass the resurrection of the dead, and that he, himself, should be oppressed and afflicted?" (Mosiah 13:27–35).

Amulek testified that Christ would offer "a great and last sacrifice" that would be infinite and eternal: "Therefore, it is expedient that there should be a great and last sacrifice, and then shall there be, or it is expedient there should be, a stop to the shedding of blood; then shall the law of Moses be fulfilled; yea, it shall be all fulfilled, every jot and tittle, and none shall have passed away" (Alma 34:13).

NEPHITE PROPHETS AND THE LAW OF MOSES

Book of Mormon prophets clearly understood the relationship between the law of Moses and the coming of Christ, which Nephi clearly stated: "For we labor diligently to write, to persuade our children, and also our brethren, to believe in Christ, and to be reconciled to God; for we know that it is by grace that we are saved, after all we can do.

"And, notwithstanding we believe in Christ, we keep the law of Moses, and look forward with steadfastness unto Christ, until the law shall be fulfilled. For, for this end was the law given; wherefore the law hath become dead unto us, and we are made alive in Christ because of our faith; yet we keep the law because of the commandments.

"And we talk of Christ, we rejoice in Christ, we preach of Christ, we prophesy of Christ, and we write according to our prophecies, that our children may know to what source they may look for a remission of their sins" (2 Nephi 25:23–26).

When Christ appeared to the Nephites, he confirmed the teachings of their prophets concerning the law of Moses being but a forerunner to the infinite and eternal sacrifice of the Son of God: "Think not that I am come to destroy the law or the prophets. I am not come to destroy but to fulfil; for verily I say unto you, one jot nor one tittle hath not passed away from the law, but in me it hath all been fulfilled" (3 Nephi 12:17–18).

"Therefore those things which were of old time, which were under the law, in me are all fulfilled. Old things are done away, and all things have become new. Therefore I would that ye should be perfect even as I, or your Father who is in heaven is perfect" (3 Nephi 12:46–48).

"Behold, I say unto you that the law is fulfilled that was given unto Moses. Behold, I am he that gave the law, and I am he who covenanted with my people Israel; therefore, the law in me is fulfilled, for I have come to fulfil the law; therefore it hath an end.

"Behold, I do not destroy the prophets, for as many as have not been fulfilled in me, verily I say unto you, shall all be fulfilled. And because I said unto you that old things have passed away, I do not destroy that which hath been spoken concerning things which are to come. For behold, the covenant which I have made with my people is not all fulfilled; but the law which was given unto Moses hath an end in me.

"Behold, I am the law, and the light. Look unto me, and endure to the end, and ye shall live; for unto him that endureth to the end will I give eternal life" (3 Nephi 15:4–9).

Of these things, President John Taylor wrote: "This Mosaic law, with all its duties, observances, ceremonies and sacrifices, continued in force until Christ's death.

"The time having come when the great atonement should be made by the offering up of Himself, Christ told Peter and John to go and prepare a place where He might, according to His custom, eat the Passover with His disciples. Eat what with His disciples? The Passover. Was it the Passover, or the Sacrament of the Lord's Supper? The Lord, in Egypt, passed by, or passed over the houses of the Israelites whose door posts had been sprinkled with the blood of the lamb sacrificed for that purpose; and the Israelites were commanded to observe this Passover in all their generations. Jesus, in compliance with this command, directed that a place be made ready where He might eat the Passover with His Apostles; for He, the great prototype, was going to offer up Himself as a lamb without spot or blemish: not only for the Israelites, but for all nations, for every people, kindred, and tongue under the face of the whole heavens: 'For God so loved the world, that he gave his only begotten Son, that whosoever believeth in him should not perish, but have everlasting life. For God sent not his Son into the world to condemn the world; but that the world through him might be saved' [John 3:16–17].

"But previous to the offering up of Himself, as the great expiatory sacrifice, having fulfilled the law and made it honorable, and having introduced the Gospel, He met with His disciples, as already noticed, to eat the Passover. He then told them, 'With desire I have desired to eat this passover with you before I suffer' [Luke 22:15]. To eat what with you? The Passover. To eat what with you? The Sacrament of the Lord's Supper. Thus He [ate] both, for the two ceremonies centered in Him, He was the embodiment of both, He was the Being provided before the foundation of the earth, and prophesied of by men of God throughout all the preceding ages; and also on account of whom the sacrifices were offered up by all the servants of the Lord, from the fall of Adam to that time; and all the various atonements heretofore offered pointed to Him, for whom they were all made and in whom they all centered. On the other hand, He it was who introduced the more perfect law, and offering Himself once for all, an infinite atonement, He, through this sacrifice, accomplished that which was designed by the Almighty before the world was, and of which the blood of bullocks, of goats and of lambs was merely the shadow.

"In view of what was almost immediately to take place, He instituted the sacrament of the Lord's Supper in commemoration of this great crowning act of redemption. When at the table, 'He took bread, and gave thanks, and brake it, and gave unto them, saying, This is my body which is given for you: this do in remembrance of me' [Luke 22:19]; afterwards, 'He took the cup, and gave thanks, and gave it to them saying, Drink ye all of it; for this is my blood of the new testament which is shed for many for the remission of sins' [Matthew 26:27–28].

"In reality, this act of the atonement was the fulfilment of the sacrifices, of the prophesying, of the Passover, and of all the leading, prominent acts of the Patriarchs and Prophets relating thereto; and having performed this, the past and the future both centered in Him. Did these worthies offer sacrifices? They prefigured His appearing and atonement. Did they prophesy? It was of Him, for the testimony of Jesus is the spirit of prophecy. Did they keep the Passover? He Himself was the great expiatory offering. Were the people called upon afterwards to commemorate this event? They did it in remembrance of Him, as a great memorial among all of His disciples in all nations, throughout all time; of the sacrifice of His broken body and spilt blood; the antitype of the sacrificial lamb slain at the time of the Passover; of Him; as being the Mediator, the Messiah, the Christ, the Alpha and Omega, the Beginning and the End: the Son of the living God.

"As from the commencement of the world to the time when the Passover was instituted, sacrifices had been offered as a memorial or type of the sacrifice of the Son of God; so from the time of the Passover until that time when He came to offer up Himself, these sacrifices and types and shadows had been carefully observed by

Prophets and Patriarchs; according to the command given to Moses and other followers of the Lord. So also did He Himself fulfil this requirement, and kept the Passover as did others; and now we, after the great sacrifice has been offered, partake of the Sacrament of the Lord's Supper in remembrance thereof. Thus this act was the great connecting link between the past and future; thus He fulfilled the law, met the demands of justice, and obeyed the requirements of His Heavenly Father, although laboring under the weight of the sins of the world, and the terrible expiation which He had to make, when, sweating great drops of blood, He cried: 'Father, if it be possible let this cup pass from me; nevertheless not my will but thine be done,' and when expiring in agony upon the cross He cried, 'It is finished,' and gave up the ghost."[5]

THE SACRAMENT TODAY

Today we are commanded to partake of the sacrament (D&C 59:9–12). This ordinance is patterned after the sacrament of the Lord's Supper introduced by Jesus to the Twelve at the Passover meal (Luke 22:15–20). After Christ introduced the sacrament to the Twelve, took upon himself the sins of all mankind in Gethsemane, and allowed himself to be lifted upon the cross to be crucified, the requirement of sacrifice by the shedding of blood under the law of Moses ceased. The modern-day ordinance of the sacrament, humbly and reverently attended to by Aaronic Priesthood holders, provides an opportunity for each of us to offer a personal sacrifice of a broken heart and a contrite spirit to Christ for his infinite and eternal sacrifice on our behalf.

NOTES

1. Bruce R. McConkie, *Mormon Doctrine*, 2d ed. (Salt Lake City: Bookcraft, 1966), 664–65.

2. John Taylor, *The Mediation and Atonement* (Salt Lake City: Deseret News, 1882), 139–41.

3. McConkie, *Mormon Doctrine*, 665.

4. Taylor, *Mediation and Atonement*, 106.

5. Taylor, *Mediation and Atonement*, 124–27.

IV
THE CREATION OF THE EARTH AND THE FALL OF MAN

It is important to understand the relationship of the law of Moses and the principle of sacrifice to the plan of redemption. It is just as important to understand the creation of the earth, the placement of Adam and Eve in the Garden of Eden, and the result of Adam and Eve's transgression in the garden. Their transgression is known as the Fall (2 Nephi 9:6).

Outside Latter-day Saint circles, Jesus Christ's creation of the heavens and earth and their purpose in the plan of redemption remain a mystery. Creative and well-meaning persons continue to postulate on the Creation. Some acknowledge divine intervention, while others advocate the Creation as the result of a "Big Bang" where "something" resulted in the Creation.

The scriptures, especially the additional scriptures available to members of the Church, provide revealed knowledge on why the earth was created, the purpose for placing God's children on the earth, and how those children can return, following physical death, to a loving Father in Heaven. The pivotal role of Adam and Eve in the Garden of Eden, the commandments they received, their transgression, and the results of their actions on all mankind are not mysteries. They must be understood in order for us to know and appreciate the Atonement.

One of the many marvelous stories in the Book of Mormon is the account of Aaron and Lamoni's father. The proud and haughty king sought confirmation from Aaron that there was a God, that he created all things, and that he was the eternal ruler of the earth. Aaron humbly taught the king about the plan of redemption, including the Atonement.

"And it came to pass that when Aaron saw that the king would believe his words, he began from the creation of Adam, reading the scriptures unto the king—how God created man after his own image, and that God gave him commandments, and that because of transgression, man had fallen.

"And Aaron did expound unto him the scriptures from the creation of Adam, laying the fall of man before him, and their carnal state and also the plan of redemption, which was prepared from the foundation of the world, through Christ, for all whosoever would believe on his name.

"And since man had fallen he could not merit anything of himself; but the sufferings and death of Christ atone for their sins, through faith and repentance, and so forth; and that he breaketh the bands of death, that the grave shall have no victory, and that the sting of death should be swallowed up in the hopes of glory; and Aaron did expound all these things unto the king" (Alma 22:12–14).

THE CREATION AND THE FALL

An understanding of the Atonement presumes an understanding of the creation of the world, the circumstances surrounding the placement of Adam and Eve in the Garden of Eden, and the subsequent fall of man. In discussing the Atonement, Elder Bruce R. McConkie said: "The three greatest events that ever have occurred or ever will occur in all eternity are these:

"1. The creation of the heavens and the earth, of man, and of all forms of life;

"2. The fall of man, of all forms of life, and of the earth itself from their primeval and paradisiacal state to their present mortal state; and

"3. The infinite and eternal atonement, which ransoms man, all living things, and the earth also from their fallen state so that the salvation of the earth and of all living things may be completed.

"These three divine events—the three pillars of eternity—are inseparably woven together into one grand tapestry known as the eternal plan of salvation. We view the atonement of the Lord Jesus Christ as the center and core and heart of revealed religion. It brings to pass the immortality and eternal life of man. Salvation is in Christ."[1]

PRE-EARTH LIFE

In the pre-earth life, before the creation of the earth, we lived with our Father in Heaven. We were spirits. He possessed a glorified body of flesh and bones. He was perfect. Because we desired to be like our Heavenly Father, he presented a plan that would make this possible.

His plan envisioned a physical experience during which we would be tested and subjected to mortal experiences. We would be separated from our Father. We would walk by faith, and we would have agency. Those who chose wisely, obeyed the commandments, and endured to the end could return to the Father. All others would be damned to one extent or another.

Lucifer offered to carry out the Father's plan but with significant and unacceptable changes. He wanted all the glory, and he wanted to force us all to return to the Father's presence by denying us agency. The Father rejected Satan's offer.

"And I, the Lord God, spake unto Moses, saying: That Satan, whom thou hast commanded in the name of mine Only Begotten, is the same which was from the beginning, and he came before me, saying—Behold, here am I, send me, I will be thy son, and I will redeem all mankind, that one soul shall not be lost, and surely I will do it; wherefore give me thine honor.

"But, behold, my Beloved Son, which was my Beloved and Chosen from the beginning, said unto me—Father, thy will be done, and the glory be thine forever.

"Wherefore, because that Satan rebelled against me, and sought to destroy the agency of man, which I, the Lord God, had given him, and also, that I should give unto him mine own power; by the power of mine Only Begotten, I caused that he should be cast down; and he became Satan, yea, even the devil, the father of all lies, to deceive and to blind men, and to lead them captive at his will, even as many as would not hearken unto my voice" (Moses 4:1–4).

THE ROLE OF JESUS CHRIST

Christ offered to do the will of the Father, giving all the honor and glory to the Father. The Father accepted Christ's offering.

Abraham wrote: "Now the Lord had shown unto me, Abraham, the intelligences that were organized before the world was; and among all these there were many of the noble and great ones; and God saw these souls that they were good, and he stood in the midst of them, and he said: These I will make my rulers; for he stood among those that were spirits, and he saw that they were good; and he said unto me: Abraham, thou art one of them; thou wast chosen before thou wast born.

"And there stood one among them that was like unto God, and he said unto those who were with him: We will go down, for there is space there, and we will take of these materials, and we will make an earth whereon these may dwell;

"And we will prove them herewith, to see if they will do all things whatsoever the Lord their God shall command them; And they who keep their first estate shall be added upon; and they who keep not their first estate shall not have glory in the same kingdom with those who keep their first estate; and they who keep their second estate shall have glory added upon their heads for ever and ever.

"And the Lord said: Whom shall I send? And one answered like unto the Son of Man: Here am I, send me. And another answered and said: Here am I, send me. And the Lord said: I will send the first" (Abraham 3:22–27).

THE COUNCIL IN HEAVEN

President John Taylor beautifully described the proceedings of this important council: "It is consistent to believe that at this Council in the heavens the plan that should be adopted in relation to the sons of God who were then spirits, and had not yet obtained tabernacles, was duly considered. For, in view of the creation of the world and the placing of men upon it, whereby it would be possible for them to obtain tabernacles, and in those tabernacles obey laws of life, and with them again be exalted among the Gods, we are told, that at that time, 'the morning stars sang together, and all the sons of God shouted for joy' [Job 38:7]. The question then arose, how, and upon what principle, should the salvation, exaltation and eternal glory of God's sons be brought about? It is evident that at that Council certain plans had been proposed and discussed, and that after a full discussion of those principles, and the declaration of the Father's will pertaining to His design, Lucifer came before the Father, with a plan of his own, saying, 'Behold, [here am] I, send me, I will be thy Son, and I will redeem all mankind, that one soul shall not be lost, and surely I will do it; wherefore, give me thine honor' [Moses 4:1]. But Jesus, on hearing this statement made by Lucifer, said, 'Father, thy will be done, and the glory be thine forever' [Moses 4:2]. From these remarks made by the well beloved Son, we should naturally infer that in the discussion of this subject the Father had made known His will and developed His plan and design pertaining to these matters, and all that His well beloved Son wanted to do was to carry out the will of His Father, as it would appear had been before expressed. He also wished the glory to be given to His Father, who, as God the Father, and the originator and designer of the plan, had a right to all the honor and glory. But Lucifer wanted to introduce a plan contrary to the will of his Father, and then wanted His honor, and said: 'I will save every soul of man, wherefore give me thine honor' [Moses 4:1]. He wanted to go contrary to the will of his Father, and presumptuously sought to deprive man of his free agency, thus making him a serf, and placing him in a position in which it was impossible for him to obtain that exaltation which God designed should be man's, through obedience to the law which He had suggested; and again, Lucifer wanted the honor and power of his Father, to enable him to carry out principles which were contrary to the Father's wish. . . .

"From the above we gather: First, that the proposition of Lucifer was an act of rebellion 'against me'—God.

"Second, that God had already decreed that man should have his free agency, and this agency had been given to him by the Lord, as it is said, 'which I, the Lord God, had given him.'

40

"Third, that Lucifer coveted and asked for a power which was the prerogative of the Almighty and alone belonged to God; and which He called 'mine own power.'

"Fourth, that for this rebellion Lucifer was cast out and became Satan.

"Fifth, that the power by which he was cast out, was by a certain power or Priesthood which had been conferred by God on His Only Begotten; for he said, 'By the power of mine Only Begotten I caused that he should be cast down.'

"Sixth, that being cast down and becoming Satan, 'even the devil, the father of lies,' his office was to deceive and to blind men; as it is stated, 'to deceive, and to blind men, and to lead them captive at his will, even as many as would not hearken unto my voice [Moses 4:3–4].'"[2]

In fulfillment of the statement and direction of the Father that "we will go down, for there is space there, and we will take of these materials, and we will make an earth whereon these may dwell" (Abraham 3:24), our earth was created or organized.

THE CREATION

The scriptures speak of the Creation taking place during six periods of time (Abraham 4–5; Moses 2–3; Genesis 1). Elder McConkie said our knowledge of the Creation comes through revelation: "Mankind's knowledge of the creation of the heavens and the earth, and of life in all its forms and varieties, comes by revelation from the Creator himself. The Lord has revealed only that portion of eternal truth relative to the creation of all things that finite minds are capable of understanding. He has given man only what he needs to know to comprehend the true doctrine of the fall, and thus to gain that salvation which comes because of the fall. There are various man-made, speculative theories about the creation. That these theories do not accord with the revealed word and that they change with every wind that blows is well known. All of this is part of the divine design. Each person is free to choose his beliefs with reference to all things, the creation included. Proper choices enable him to build a house of faith that will shelter him from every wind of false doctrine that may chance to blow in his day."[3]

It is clear that the purpose of the creation of heaven and earth was to fulfill the purposes of God Almighty with respect to his children.

MOSES TESTIFIES OF THE CREATION

In a revelation to Moses, the Lord God spoke the following words: "For behold, this is my work and my glory—to bring to pass the immortality and eternal life of man" (Moses 1:39). The "eternal life of man" as spoken of in this scripture is not guaranteed by the Atonement, but the Atonement makes eternal life possible.

In a vision given to him after he was caught up in a high mountain, Moses "saw God face to face, and he talked with him, and the glory of God was upon Moses; therefore Moses could endure his presence.

"And God spake unto Moses, saying: Behold, I am the Lord God Almighty, and Endless is my name; for I am without beginning of days or end of years; and is not this endless? And, behold, thou art my son; wherefore look, and I will show thee the workmanship of mine hands; but not all, for my works are without end, and also my words, for they never cease.

"Wherefore, no man can behold all my works, except he behold all my glory; and no man can behold all my glory, and afterwards remain in the flesh on the earth. And I have a work for thee, Moses, my son; and thou art in the similitude of mine Only Begotten; and mine Only Begotten is and shall be the Savior, for he is full of grace and truth; but there is no God beside me, and all things are present with me, for I know them all. And now, behold, this one thing I show unto thee, Moses, my son, for thou art in the world, and now I show it unto thee.

"And it came to pass that Moses looked, and beheld the world upon which he was created; and Moses beheld the world and the ends thereof, and all the children of men which are, and which were created; of the same he greatly marveled and wondered" (Moses 1:1–8).

"And it came to pass, as the voice was still speaking, Moses cast his eyes and beheld the earth, yea, even all of it; and there was not a particle of it which he did not behold, discerning it by the spirit of God. And he beheld also the inhabitants thereof, and there was not a soul which he beheld not; and he discerned them by the Spirit of God; and their numbers were great, even numberless as the sand upon the sea shore.

"And he beheld many lands; and each land was called earth, and there were inhabitants on the face thereof. And it came to pass that Moses called upon God, saying: Tell me, I pray thee, why these things are so, and by what thou madest them?

"And behold, the glory of the Lord was upon Moses, so that Moses stood in the presence of God, and talked with him face to face. And the Lord God said unto Moses: For mine own purpose have I made these things. Here is wisdom and it remaineth in me.

"And by the word of my power, have I created them, which is mine Only Begotten Son, who is full of grace and truth. And worlds without number have I created; and I also created them for mine own purpose; and by the Son I created them, which is mine Only Begotten. And the first man of all men have I called Adam, which is many.

"But only an account of this earth, and the inhabitants thereof, give I unto you. For behold, there are many worlds that have passed away by the word of my power. And there are many that now stand, and innumerable are they unto man; but all things are numbered unto me, for they are mine and I know them" (Moses 1:27–35).

THE CREATION OF MAN AND WOMAN

The concluding act of the Creation was the creation of man and woman: "And God said, Let us make man in our image, after our likeness: and let them have dominion over the fish of the sea, and over the fowl of the air, and over the cattle, and over all the earth, and over every creeping thing that creepeth upon the earth. So God created man in his own image, in the image of God created he him; male and female created he them" (Genesis 1:26–27).

The Book of Mormon provides the clearest understanding of the condition of Adam and Eve in the Garden of Eden: "After the Lord God sent our first parents forth from the garden of Eden, to till the ground, from whence they were taken—yea, he drew out the man, and he placed at the east end of the garden of Eden, cherubim, and a flaming sword which turned every way, to keep the tree of life—

"Now, we see that the man had become as God, knowing good and evil; and lest he should put forth his hand, and take also of the tree of life, and eat and live forever, the Lord God placed cherubim and the flaming sword, that he should not partake of the fruit—And thus we see, that there was a time granted unto man to repent, yea, a probationary time, a time to repent and serve God.

"For behold, if Adam had put forth his hand immediately, and partaken of the tree of life, he would have lived forever, according to the word of God, having no space for repentance; yea, and also the word of God would have been void, and the great plan of salvation would have been frustrated. But behold, it was appointed unto man to die—therefore, as they were cut off from the tree of life they should be cut off from the face of the earth—and man became lost forever, yea, they became fallen man.

"And now, ye see by this that our first parents were cut off both temporally and spiritually from the presence of the Lord; and thus we see they became subjects to follow after their own will. Now behold, it was not expedient that man should be reclaimed from this temporal death, for that would destroy the great plan of happiness. Therefore, as the soul could never die, and the fall had brought upon all mankind a spiritual death as well as a temporal, that is, they were cut off from the presence of the Lord, it was expedient that mankind should be reclaimed from this spiritual death.

"Therefore, as they had become carnal, sensual, and devilish, by nature, this probationary state became a state for them to prepare; it became a preparatory state. And now remember, my son, if it were not for the plan of redemption, (laying it aside) as soon as they were dead their souls were miserable, being cut off from the presence of the Lord" (Alma 42:2–11).

How grateful we ought to be for having the privilege of living in "this probationary state." It was never intended that this earth-life experience be the end of our existence. Cherubim, prohibiting Adam and Eve from partaking of the tree of life, gave all mankind a time to repent and a time to serve God. Accordingly, the "great plan of salvation," or the "great plan of happiness," was not frustrated. As each one of us lives and ultimately dies, the plan is fulfilled. As difficult as the aging of the body and the onset of physical infirmities are to experience or observe in ourselves and in others, these experiences assure us that we will not live on this earth in our present physical state forever.

Father Lehi earlier taught the same principles as Alma

concerning Adam and Eve: "Wherefore, the Lord God gave unto man that he should act for himself. Wherefore, man could not act for himself save it should be that he was enticed by the one or the other.

"And I, Lehi, according to the things which I have read, must needs suppose that an angel of God, according to that which is written, had fallen from heaven; wherefore, he became a devil, having sought that which was evil before God.

"And because he had fallen from heaven, and had become miserable forever, he sought also the misery of all mankind. Wherefore, he said unto Eve, yea, even that old serpent, who is the devil, who is the father of all lies, wherefore he said: Partake of the forbidden fruit, and ye shall not die, but ye shall be as God, knowing good and evil.

"And after Adam and Eve had partaken of the forbidden fruit they were driven out of the garden of Eden, to till the earth. And they have brought forth children; yea, even the family of all the earth.

"And the days of the children of men were prolonged, according to the will of God, that they might repent while in the flesh; wherefore, their state became a state of probation, and their time was lengthened, according to the commandments which the Lord God gave unto the children of men. For he gave commandment that all men must repent; for he showed unto all men that they were lost, because of the transgression of their parents.

"And now, behold, if Adam had not transgressed he would not have fallen, but he would have remained in the garden of Eden. And all things which were created must have remained in the same state in which they were after they were created; and they must have remained forever, and had no end.

"And they would have had no children; wherefore they would

have remained in a state of innocence, having no joy, for they knew no misery; doing no good, for they knew no sin. But behold, all things have been done in the wisdom of him who knoweth all things. Adam fell that men might be; and men are, that they might have joy" (2 Nephi 2:16–25).

ADAM AND EVE CAST OUT OF THE GARDEN

Antionah, a chief ruler, asked Alma, "What does the scripture mean, which saith that God placed cherubim and a flaming sword on the east of the garden of Eden, lest our first parents should enter and partake of the fruit of the tree of life, and live forever? And thus we see that there was no possible chance that they should live forever. Now Alma said unto him: . . . We see that Adam did fall by the partaking of the forbidden fruit, according to the word of God; and thus we see, that by his fall, all mankind became a lost and fallen people.

"And now behold, I say unto you that if it had been possible for Adam to have partaken of the fruit of the tree of life at that time, there would have been no death, and the word would have been void, making God a liar, for he said: If thou eat thou shalt surely die.

"And we see that death comes upon mankind, yea, the death which has been spoken of by Amulek, which is the temporal death; nevertheless there was a space granted unto man in which he might repent; therefore this life became a probationary state; a time to prepare to meet God; a time to prepare for that endless state which has been spoken of by us, which is after the resurrection of the dead.

"Now, if it had not been for the plan of redemption, which was laid from the foundation of the world, there could have been no resurrection of the dead; but there was a plan of redemption laid, which shall bring to pass the resurrection of the dead, of which has been spoken.

"And now behold, if it were possible that our first parents could have gone forth and partaken of the tree of life they would have been forever miserable, having no preparatory state; and thus the plan of redemption would have been frustrated, and the word of God would have been void, taking none effect. But behold, it was not so; but it was appointed unto men that they must die; and after death, they must come to judgment, even that same judgment of which we have spoken, which is the end" (Alma 12:21–27).

Elder McConkie also provided insight on what happened to Adam and Eve: "We do not know how the fall was accomplished any more than we know how the Lord caused the earth to come into being and to spin through the heavens in its paradisiacal state. We have been given only enough information about the creation and the fall to enable us to understand the purposes of the Lord, to exercise faith in him, and to gain our salvation.

"As to the fall, the scriptures set forth that there were in the Garden of Eden two trees. One was the tree of life, which figuratively refers to eternal life; the other was the tree of knowledge of good and evil, which figuratively refers to how and why and in what manner mortality and all that appertains to it came into being. 'Of every tree of the garden thou mayest freely eat,' the Lord told our first parents, 'but of the tree of knowledge of good and evil, thou shalt not eat of it, nevertheless, thou mayest choose for thyself, for it is given unto thee; but, remember that I forbid it, for in the day thou eatest thereof thou shalt surely die.' (Moses 3:16–17.)

"Eve partook without full understanding; Adam partook knowing that unless he did so, he and Eve could not have children and fulfill the commandment they had received to multiply and replenish the earth. After they had thus complied with whatever the law was that brought mortality into being, the Lord said to Eve: 'I will greatly multiply thy sorrow and thy conception. In sorrow thou shalt bring forth children, and thy desire shall be to thy husband, and he shall rule over thee.' To Adam the decree came: 'Cursed shall be the ground for thy sake; in sorrow shalt thou eat of it all the days of thy life. Thorns also, and thistles shall it bring forth to thee.' Thus the paradisiacal earth was cursed; thus it fell; and thus it became as it now is.

"Adam was then told that he would surely die, returning through death to the dust whence his physical body had come. And then the Lord said to his Only Begotten: 'Behold, the man is become as one of us to know good and evil; and now lest he put forth his hand and partake also of the tree of life, and eat and live forever [in his sins!], therefore, I, the Lord God, will send him forth from the Garden of Eden, to till the ground from whence he was taken.' (Moses 4:22–29.) Such is the ancient account of the fall."[4]

Following their departure from the Garden of Eden, Adam and Eve came to know and understand that their transgression of the law would result in the fulfillment of a greater law—the "great plan of happiness."

"And after many days an angel of the Lord appeared unto Adam, saying: Why dost thou offer sacrifices unto the Lord? And Adam said unto him: I know not, save the Lord commanded me.

"And then the angel spake, saying: This thing is a similitude of the sacrifice of the Only Begotten of the Father, which is full of grace and truth. Wherefore, thou shalt do all that thou doest in the name of the Son, and thou shalt repent and call upon God in the name of the Son forevermore.

"And in that day the Holy Ghost fell upon Adam, which beareth record of the Father and the Son, saying: I am the Only Begotten of the Father from the beginning, henceforth and forever, that as thou hast fallen thou mayest be redeemed, and all mankind, even as many as will" (Moses 5:6–9).

The knowledge of the opportunity for all mankind to be redeemed came as a marvelous blessing and revelation to Adam and Eve. Adam said, "For because of my transgression my eyes are opened, and in this life I shall have joy, and again in the flesh I shall see God" (Moses 5:10). Eve uttered a similar acclamation: "Were it not for our transgression we never should have had seed, and never should have known good and evil, and the joy of our redemption" (Moses 5:11).

President John Taylor spoke of the blessings gained as a result of the transgression of Adam and Eve: "Thus we find: Firstly. That Adam and Eve both considered that they had gained, instead of suffered loss, through their disobedience to that law; for they made the statement, that if it had not been for their transgression they never would 'have known good and evil.' And again, they would have been incapable of increase; and without that increase the designs of God in relation to the formation of the earth and man could not have been accomplished; for one great object of the creation of the world was the propagation of the human species, that bodies might be prepared for those spirits who already existed, and who, when they saw the earth formed, shouted for joy.

"Secondly. By pursuing the course they did, through the atonement, they would see God as they had done before; and furthermore, they would be capable of exaltation, which was made possible only through their fall, and the atonement of Jesus Christ; and also, they might have the comforting influence of the Spirit of God, and His guidance and direction here, as well as eternal lives and exaltations in the world to come."[5]

THE FALL OF MAN

The term "the Fall" or "the Fall of Adam" refers to the condition or change that came upon Adam and Eve as a result of their transgression in the Garden of Eden. Jacob said that "the fall came by reason of transgression; and because man became fallen they were cut off from the presence of the Lord" (2 Nephi 9:6). Regarding Adam's transgression, the second article of faith says, "We believe that men will be punished for their own sins, and not for Adam's transgression."

The Doctrine and Covenants helps us understand the effect of Adam's transgression: "Wherefore, it came to pass that the devil tempted Adam, and he partook of the forbidden fruit and transgressed the commandment, wherein he became subject to the will of the devil, because he yielded unto temptation.

"Wherefore, I, the Lord God, caused that he should be cast out from the Garden of Eden, from my presence, because of his transgression, wherein he became spiritually dead, which is the first death, even that same death which is the last death, which is spiritual, which shall be pronounced upon the wicked when I shall say: Depart, ye cursed.

"But, behold, I say unto you that I, the Lord God, gave unto Adam and unto his seed, that they should not die as to the temporal death, until I, the Lord God, should send forth angels to declare unto them repentance and redemption, through faith on the name of mine Only Begotten Son.

"And thus did I, the Lord God, appoint unto man the days of his probation—that by his natural death he might be raised in immortality unto eternal life, even as many as would believe" (D&C 29:40–43).

UNDERSTANDING THE FALL

Elder James E. Talmage provided us with understanding of the immediate result of the Fall: "The immediate result of the fall was the substitution of mortality, with all its attendant frailties, for the vigor of the primeval deathless state. Adam felt directly the effects of transgression in finding a barren and dreary earth, with a relatively sterile soil, instead of the beauty and fruitfulness of Eden. In place of pleasing and useful plants, thorns and thistles sprang up; and the man had to labor arduously, under the conditions of physical fatigue and suffering, to cultivate the soil that he might obtain necessary food. Upon Eve fell the penalty of bodily infirmity; pains and sorrows, which since have been regarded as the natural lot of womankind, came upon her, and she was made subject to her husband's authority. Having lost their sense of former innocence they became ashamed of their nakedness, and the Lord made for them garments of skins. Upon both the man and the woman was visited the penalty of spiritual death; for in that very day they were banished from Eden and cast out from the presence of the Lord. The serpent, having served the purposes of Satan, was made a subject of divine displeasure, being doomed to crawl forever in the dust, and to suffer from the enmity which it was decreed should be placed in the hearts of Eve's children."[6]

The effect of the Fall of Adam was death—spiritual death and physical death. Elder McConkie wrote: "The fall of Adam brought temporal and spiritual death into the world. Temporal death is the natural death; it occurs when body and spirit separate, thus leaving the body to return to the dust whence it came. Spiritual death is to be cast out of the presence of the Lord and to die as pertaining to the things of righteousness. Adam died spiritually when he was cast out of the heavenly presence found in the garden, and he remained spiritually dead until he repented and was born again through baptism and the receipt of the Holy Spirit. Having thus the companionship of the Holy Ghost, he became alive in Christ and was again guided and directed from on high. He was again in the presence of the Lord. Adam died temporally when his spirit separated from his mortal body."[7]

The Lord revealed to Moses the warning given to Adam: "For in the day thou eatest thereof thou shalt surely die" (Moses 3:17). Adam died physically 930 years after the Fall.

The Fall included the breaking of a law, for which a penalty was affixed. Overcoming the effects of the Fall is the mission of Jesus Christ. While a visual image of "a fall" connotes someone or something falling downward, a more accurate understanding of the Fall was reported by B. H. Roberts. He quoted a Protestant dictionary of Christianity that said, "In Mormon teaching, further, the fall of man is considered a fall upward!"[8]

Hope through Christ is found in the writings of Moroni: "Behold, he created Adam, and by Adam came the fall of man. And because of the fall of man came Jesus Christ, even the Father and the Son; and because of Jesus Christ came the redemption of man.

"And because of the redemption of man, which came by Jesus Christ, they are brought back into the presence of the Lord; yea, this is wherein all men are redeemed, because the death of Christ bringeth to pass the resurrection, which bringeth to pass a redemption from an endless sleep, from which sleep all men shall be awakened by the power of God when the trump shall sound; and they shall come forth, both small and great, and all shall stand before his bar, being redeemed and loosed from this eternal band of death, which death is a temporal death" (Mormon 9:12–13).

NOTES

1. Bruce R. McConkie, A New Witness for the Articles of Faith (Salt Lake City: Deseret Book, 1985), 81.

2. John Taylor, The Mediation and Atonement (Salt Lake City: Deseret News, 1882), 93–94, 98.

3. McConkie, New Witness, 82.

4. McConkie, New Witness, 85–86.

5. Taylor, *Mediation and Atonement*, 130.

6. James E. Talmage, *The Articles of Faith* (Salt Lake City: Deseret Book, 1984), 61.

7. McConkie, *New Witness*, 86–87.

8. B. H. Roberts, *The Truth, the Way, the Life—An Elementary Treatise on Theology*, ed. John W. Welch (Provo, Utah: BYU Studies, 1994), cxxxix.

V
THE MISSION OF JESUS CHRIST

As we gain an understanding of the Creation and the Fall and of how the Fall affects every person who is born on earth, we are led toward Jesus Christ and his mission. Like a light that shines so brightly that it cannot be dimmed, hidden, or ignored, Jesus Christ is the only means by which the Fall can be overcome.

Why did Christ come to earth? What did Christ do that compensated for the results of the Fall? How did Christ provide the means of overcoming physical and spiritual death?

The scriptures are clear and unequivocal in testifying of the mission of Jesus Christ. True believers and possessors of truth should know the individual responsibility God's children have to progress in this life so that they may return to their Heavenly Father.

We will next examine the true doctrine of why Christ came to earth, why he established his Church, what happened in the Garden of Gethsemane the night before the Crucifixion, and the results of the Crucifixion. The special significance of the Resurrection of Christ and its meaning for all mankind are essential to our understanding of the Atonement.

"That he came into the world, even Jesus, to be crucified for the world, and to bear the sins of the world, and to sanctify the world, and to cleanse it from all unrighteousness; that through him all might be saved whom the Father had put into his power and made by him" (D&C 76:41–42).

The Apostle Paul explained to the Saints in Corinth a major purpose of the mission of Christ: "But now is Christ risen from the dead, and become the firstfruits of them that slept. For since by man came death, by man came also the resurrection of the dead. For as in Adam all die, even so in Christ shall all be made alive" (1 Corinthians 15:20–22).

One of the main purposes for the coming of Christ to earth was to replace physical and spiritual death with life.

OVERCOMING PHYSICAL DEATH

Physical death is the separation of the spirit from the physical body. At death, the body is laid in the ground, and the righteous spirit is received into a state of happiness called paradise (Alma 40:11–12). Those who are wicked and choose evil rather than good while in mortality go to a place within the postmortal spirit world referred to as "darkness" (Alma 40:13–14) or spirit prison. From among the righteous in paradise, missionaries are selected to teach the gospel to those in spirit prison (D&C 138:30).

It was never intended that the spirit and the body remain forever separated. After all, "the spirit and the body are the soul of man" (D&C 88:15). Man was created in the image and likeness of God (Genesis 1:26–27), who is a glorified personage possessing a spirit and a perfected physical body (Joseph Smith—History 1:17). When we, as personages of spirit, were in the pre-earthly existence, we recognized that God had a spirit and a perfected body. Could we, in a spirit state only, become like God? No. We had to gain physical bodies through birth on a physical earth. That process began when Adam and Eve became the first physical beings on earth, possessing bodies that housed their spirits (Moses 3:7). When Adam and Eve died physically, as does every other human being, their spirits were separated from their bodies.

One of the missions of Jesus Christ was to overcome physical death by providing a literal and universal resurrection for all mankind. The word *resurrection* has various origins of similar meaning. From the Middle English root *resurrectio*, it means the "act of rising from the dead." In Latin it means "to rise again."[1]

Two verses in the Doctrine and Covenants provide the answer to physical death: "And the resurrection from the dead is the redemption of the soul. And the redemption of the soul is through him that quickeneth all things, in whose bosom it is decreed that the poor and the meek of the earth shall inherit it" (D&C 88:16–17).

Redemption is the act or process of redeeming. The word *redeem* comes from the Latin *redimere*, which means to take, buy, buy back, or repurchase. Another definition is "to free from captivity by payment of ransom."[2]

OVERCOMING SPIRITUAL DEATH

One of the consequences of the Fall of Adam was expulsion from the beautiful and peaceful Garden of Eden: "Therefore the Lord God sent him forth from the garden of Eden, to till the ground from whence he was taken. So he drove out the man; and he placed at the east of the garden of Eden Cherubims, and a flaming sword which turned every way, to keep the way of the tree of life" (Genesis 3:23–24).

"And I, the Lord God, said unto the serpent: Because thou hast done this thou shalt be cursed above all cattle, and above every beast of the field; upon thy belly shalt thou go, and dust shalt thou eat all the days of thy life; . . .

"Therefore I, the Lord God, will send him forth from the Garden of Eden, to till the ground from whence he was taken; For as I, the Lord God, liveth, even so my words cannot return void, for as they go forth out of my mouth they must be fulfilled.

"So I drove out the man, and I placed at the east of the Garden of Eden, cherubim and a flaming sword, which turned every way to keep the way of the tree of life" (Moses 4:20, 29–31).

In the Garden of Eden, Adam freely conversed with God (Moses 3:15–17). He gave names to the living creatures created by God (Genesis 2:19–20). He received commandments and instructions, including the commandment to not eat of the tree of knowledge of good and evil (Genesis 2:17).

After Adam and Eve transgressed the law and partook of the fruit of the tree of knowledge of good and evil, they were banished from the Garden of Eden and lost the privilege of direct and unrestrained communication with God. Thereafter, communication from God resulted from faith and sacrifice combined with heartfelt petitioning.

"And Adam and Eve, his wife, called upon the name of the Lord, and they heard the voice of the Lord from the way toward the Garden of Eden, speaking unto them, and they saw him not; for they were shut out from his presence.

"And he gave unto them commandments, that they should worship the Lord their God, and should offer the firstlings of their flocks, for an offering unto the Lord. And Adam was obedient unto the commandments of the Lord.

"And after many days an angel of the Lord appeared unto Adam, saying: Why dost thou offer sacrifices unto the Lord? And Adam said unto him: I know not, save the Lord commanded me.

And then the angel spake, saying: This thing is a similitude of the sacrifice of the Only Begotten of the Father, which is full of grace and truth. Wherefore, thou shalt do all that thou doest in the name of the Son, and thou shalt repent and call upon God in the name of the Son forevermore.

"And in that day the Holy Ghost fell upon Adam, which beareth record of the Father and the Son, saying: I am the Only Begotten of the Father from the beginning, henceforth and forever, that as thou hast fallen thou mayest be redeemed, and all mankind, even as many as will.

"And in that day Adam blessed God and was filled, and began to prophesy concerning all the families of the earth, saying: Blessed be the name of God, for because of my transgression my eyes are opened, and in this life I shall have joy, and again in the flesh I shall see God" (Moses 5:4–10).

Obedience to God, including the offering of sacrifices in "a similitude of the sacrifice of the Only Begotten of the Father," gave hope and promise to Adam and his posterity that, despite the loss of direct and continual heavenly communication, God was still there. God knew and loved Adam and Eve, and he provided a way whereby they might return to him. The promised way was through repentance and faith in Jesus Christ, who would offer the ultimate and infinite sacrifice.

Adam and Eve were "shut out from his presence." On occasion Adam's "eyes [were] opened," but the privilege of open and continual communication with God was lost. Since then, God's children have been born on this earth without a recollection of their pre-earthly existence. We do not remember our prior association with God. We have the testimony of the scriptures and prophets to teach us that we lived with him at an earlier time, but we walk by faith, which is one of the major purposes of our birth.

We live in a state of spiritual death. Our spirits are separated from God. He dwells in heaven; we live on earth. We would like to return to him, but he is clean and perfect and we are unclean and imperfect.

An important part of the mission of Jesus Christ was to help us overcome spiritual death. However, this is not an unconditional, universal gift as is the Resurrection. Each individual must qualify for the blessings of this aspect of the Atonement by choosing to comply with prescribed conditions. The law of agency applies to each man and woman.

Christ has provided a way for us to become clean again, which we call repentance and baptism. He has provided the Church and kingdom of God on earth whereby we may be taught. And he has provided ordinances and covenants that we may elect to enter into, though not all will do so. We may overcome spiritual death and return to God—through the Atonement of Jesus Christ—if we choose wisely and obey.

THE DOCTRINE

Jacob taught that the reconciliation of the physical and spiritual death can only come through the Atonement of Jesus Christ: "Wherefore, beloved brethren, be reconciled unto him through the atonement of Christ, his Only Begotten Son, and ye may obtain a resurrection, according to the power of the resurrection which is in Christ, and be presented as the first-fruits of Christ unto God, having faith, and obtained a good hope of glory in him before he manifesteth himself in the flesh.

"And now, beloved, marvel not that I tell you these things; for why not speak of the atonement of Christ, and attain to a perfect knowledge of him, as to attain to the knowledge of a resurrection and the world to come?" (Jacob 4:11–12).

Yes, why not speak of the Atonement of Christ? There truly will be a resurrection and a reuniting of the physical body with the spirit. There actually is a plan whereby we can return to God if we obey him. These things "really will be" (Jacob 4:13). All of this is made possible through the Atonement of Jesus Christ.

Jacob spoke of the "infinite" nature of the Atonement: "For as death hath passed upon all men, to fulfil the merciful plan of the great Creator, there must needs be a power of resurrection, and the resurrection must needs come unto man by reason of the fall; and the fall came by reason of transgression; and because man became fallen they were cut off from the presence of the Lord.

"Wherefore, it must needs be an infinite atonement—save it should be an infinite atonement this corruption could not put on incorruption. Wherefore, the first judgment which came upon man must needs have remained to an endless duration. And if so, this flesh must have laid down to rot and to crumble to its mother earth, to rise no more" (2 Nephi 9:6–7).

Concerning the principle taught in this scripture, President John Taylor wrote: "There is a principle developed in the above quotation to the effect that death was 'passed upon all men to fulfil the merciful plan of the great Creator;' and furthermore, that the resurrection came 'by reason of the fall.' For if man had not sinned, there would have been no death, and if Jesus had not atoned for the sin, there would have been no resurrection. Hence these things are spoken of as being according to the merciful plan of God. This corruption could not have put on incorruption, and this mortality could not have put on immortality; for, as we have elsewhere shown, man by reason of any thing that he himself could do or accomplish, could only exalt himself to the dignity and capability of man and therefore it needed the atonement of a God, before man, through the adoption, could be exalted to the Godhead.

"Again, if the body could not have been resurrected, it would have had to 'crumble to its mother earth,' and remain in that condition without the capability of ascending to the Godhead; and furthermore, not only would our bodies have lost their entity, their life and power, but the spirit also would have been placed in a state of subjection 'to that angel who fell from before the presence of the eternal God, and became the devil,' without a capability or even hope of life, salvation and exaltation, and would have been deprived of all free agency and power, and subject to the influences, dominion and eternal destruction of Lucifer, the enemy of man and of God. Hence, on this ground, and because of the terrible effects which would have resulted to humanity from the proposed plan to deprive man of his free agency, and in seeking to do away with the atonement, Lucifer was cast out of heaven, as were also those associated with him in the same diabolical plans and purposes."[3]

The Book of Mormon gives further testimony that Christ will work the mighty Atonement: "And now, behold, I will testify unto you of myself that these things are true. Behold, I say unto you, that I do know that Christ shall come among the children of men, to take upon him the transgressions of his people, and that he shall atone for the sins of the world; for the Lord God hath spoken it.

"For it is expedient that an atonement should be made; for according to the great plan of the Eternal God there must be an atonement made, or else all mankind must unavoidably perish; yea, all are hardened; yea, all are fallen and are lost, and must perish except it be through the atonement which it is expedient should be made.

"For it is expedient that there should be a great and last sacrifice; yea, not a sacrifice of man, neither of beast, neither of any manner of fowl; for it shall not be a human sacrifice; but it must be an infinite and eternal sacrifice" (Alma 34:8–10).

This beautiful scripture, the testimony of Amulek, speaks of an Atonement that is expedient—that must take place—to achieve a particular end. It refers to a "great and last sacrifice" that is "not a sacrifice of man, neither of beast, neither of any manner of fowl," thus precluding further sacrifice under the law of Moses. And it refers to the sacrifice of Jesus Christ as "infinite and eternal."

What is an "infinite and eternal sacrifice"? The words *infinite* and *eternal* could mean something that is subject to no limitation, is boundless, and is of an incalculably great number. Another definition of these two words, as provided by Amulek, describes the Atonement: "And behold, this is the whole meaning of the law, every whit pointing to that great and last sacrifice; and that great and last sacrifice will be *the Son of God*, yea, infinite and eternal.

"And thus he shall bring salvation to all those who shall believe on his name; this being the intent of this last sacrifice, to bring about the bowels of mercy, which overpowereth justice, and bringeth about means unto men that they may have faith unto repentance.

"And thus mercy can satisfy the demands of justice, and encircles them in the arms of safety, while he that exercises no faith unto repentance is exposed to the whole law of the demands of justice; therefore only unto him that has faith unto repentance is brought about the great and eternal plan of redemption" (Alma 34:14–16; emphasis added).

The "great and last sacrifice will be the Son of God, yea, infinite and eternal." Among the many names subscribed to God and his Son, Jesus Christ, are the names "infinite and eternal."

"By these things we know that there is a God in heaven, who is infinite and eternal, from everlasting to everlasting the same unchangeable God, the framer of heaven and earth, and all things which are in them; and that he created man, male and female, after his own image and in his own likeness, created he them; and gave unto them commandments that they should love and serve him, the only living and true God, and that he should be the only being whom they should worship.

"But by the transgression of these holy laws man became sensual and devilish, and became fallen man. Wherefore, the Almighty God gave his Only Begotten Son, as it is written in those scriptures which have been given of him.

"He suffered temptations but gave no heed unto them. He was crucified, died, and rose again the third day; and ascended into heaven, to sit down on the right hand of the Father, to reign with almighty power according to the will of the Father; that as many as would believe and be baptized in his holy name, and endure in faith to the end, should be saved—

"Not only those who believed after he came in the meridian of time, in the flesh, but all those from the beginning, even as many as were before he came, who believed in the words of the holy prophets, who spake as they were inspired by the gift of the Holy Ghost, who truly testified of him in all things, should have eternal life, as well as those who should come after, who should believe in the gifts and callings of God by the Holy Ghost, which beareth record of the Father and of the Son; which Father, Son, and Holy Ghost are one God, infinite and eternal, without end. Amen" (D&C 20:17–28).

The Father and the Son, who are unified, are both infinite and eternal. Nothing can be infinite and eternal unless God created it. The absolute unity by which the Father and the Son brought about the Atonement is found in Christ's prayer to the Father in the Garden of Gethsemane. Elder Bruce R. McConkie described the prayer:

"We cannot recount with surety the order in which each thing happened, nor reconstruct with certainty the sequence of Jesus' spoken words, this night in this garden—in this 'other Eden, in which the Second Adam, the Lord from heaven, bore the penalty of the first, and in obeying gained life.' [Alfred Edersheim, *The Life and Times of Jesus the Messiah*, 1883, 2:534.] What has been preserved for us is only a sliver from a great tree, only a few sentences of what was said, only a brief glimpse of what transpired. It would appear that Jesus and the disciples spent some hours there in Gethsemane; that one (or many!) angels were present; and that Jesus poured out his soul in agony as he interceded for the faithful and felt the weight of the world's sins upon his own sinless soul. There is no mystery to compare with the mystery of redemption, not even the mystery of creation. Finite minds can no more comprehend how and in what manner Jesus performed his redeeming labors than they can comprehend how matter came into being, or how Gods began to be. Perhaps the very reason Peter, James, and John slept was to enable a divine providence to withhold from their ears, and seal up from their eyes, those things which only Gods can comprehend. We do know, however, that these words were included in Jesus' prayer:

O my Father, if it be possible, let this cup pass from me: nevertheless not as I will, but as thou wilt. (Matthew.)

Abba, Father, all things are possible unto thee; take away this cup from me; nevertheless, not my will, but thine be done. (Mark.)

Father, if thou be willing, remove this cup from me: nevertheless not my will, but thine, be done. (Luke.)

"Then, as nearly as we can determine, and as Luke records: 'There appeared an angel unto him from heaven, strengthening him.' The angelic ministrant is not named. We know that on the Mount of Transfiguration 'Moses and Elias . . . appeared in glory, and spake of his decease which he should accomplish at Jerusalem'

(Luke 9:30–31); and if we might indulge in speculation, we would suggest that the angel who came into this second Eden was the same person who dwelt in the first Eden. At least Adam, who is Michael, the archangel—the head of the whole heavenly hierarchy of angelic ministrants—seems the logical one to give aid and comfort to his Lord on such a solemn occasion. Adam fell, and Christ redeemed men from the fall; theirs was a joint enterprise, both parts of which were essential for the salvation of the Father's children.

"But back to Luke. 'And being in an agony he prayed more earnestly: and his sweat was as it were great drops of blood falling down to the ground.' [Luke 22:44.] The Son of God who did all things well—whose every thought and act and deed was perfect; whose every prayer pierced the firmament and ascended to his Father—the Son of God himself (note it well) 'prayed more earnestly.' Even he reached a pinnacle of perfection in prayer that had not always been his. And as to the blood that oozed from his pores, we cannot do better than recall the words of the angelic ministrant, spoken to the Nephite [king], Benjamin: 'And lo, he shall suffer temptations, and pain of body, . . . even more than man can suffer, except it be unto death; for behold, blood cometh from every pore, so great shall be his anguish for the wickedness and the abominations of his people.' (Mosiah 3:7.)"[4]

As we ponder the mission of Jesus Christ in providing the Atonement for each of us, we should have a profound love and respect for what he did. We cannot fully understand it. It is so complex yet so simple. He died for us and provided the means to return to our Father with our resurrected bodies.

Elder McConkie, quoting Frederic W. Farrar,[5] described the suffering of Christ in the Garden of Gethsemane: "'Jesus knew that the awful hour of His deepest humiliation had arrived—that from this moment till the utterance of that great cry with which He

expired, nothing remained for Him on earth but the torture of physical pain and the poignancy of mental anguish. All that the human
frame can tolerate of suffering was to be heaped upon His shrink-
ing body; every misery that cruel and crushing insult can inflict was
to weigh heavy on His soul; and in this torment of body and agony
of soul even the high and radiant serenity of His divine spirit was
to suffer a short but terrible eclipse. Pain in its acutest sting, shame
in its most overwhelming brutality, all the burden of the sin and
mystery of man's existence in its apostasy and fall—this was what
He must now face in all its most inexplicable accumulation.' . . .

"There is no language known to mortals that can tell what
agony and suffering was his while in the Garden. Of it Farrar says:
'A grief beyond utterance, a struggle beyond endurance, a horror of
great darkness, a giddiness and stupefaction of soul overmastered
Him, as with the sinking swoon of an anticipated death. . . . How
dreadful was that paroxysm of prayer and suffering through which
He passed.' . . .

"And as to the prayer in the Garden—repeating, as it did, his
divine promise made in the councils of eternity when he was chosen for the labors and sufferings of this very hour; the divine prayer
in which he said, 'Father, thy will be done, and the glory be thine
forever' (Moses 4:2)—as to the prayer in the Garden, 'That prayer
in all its infinite reverence and awe was heard; that strong crying
and those tears were not rejected. We may not intrude too closely
into this scene. It is shrouded in a halo and a mystery into which
no footstep may penetrate. We, as we contemplate it, are like those
disciples—our senses are confused, our perceptions are not clear.
We can but enter into their amazement and sore distress. Half
waking, half oppressed with an irresistible weight of troubled slum-
ber, they only felt that they were dim witnesses of an unutterable
agony, far deeper than anything which they could fathom, as it far

transcended all that, even in our purest moments, we can pretend to understand. The place seems haunted by presences of good and evil, struggling in mighty but silent contest for the eternal victory. They see Him, before whom the demons had fled in howling terror, lying on His face upon the ground. They hear that voice wailing in murmurs of broken agony, which had commanded the wind and the sea, and they obeyed Him. The great drops of anguish which fall from Him in the deathful struggle, look to them like heavy gouts of blood.' . . . And so they were."[6]

Once again, the beautiful and inspired writings of President John Taylor help us appreciate in some small degree the suffering of Jesus Christ in Gethsemane and on the cross: "The suffering of the Son of God was not simply the suffering of personal death; for in assuming the position that He did in making an atonement for the sins of the world He bore the weight, the responsibility, and the burden of the sins of all men, which, to us, is incomprehensible. . . .

"Groaning beneath this concentrated load, this intense, incomprehensible pressure, this terrible exaction of Divine justice, from which feeble humanity shrank, and through the agony thus experienced sweating great drops of blood, He was led to exclaim, 'Father, if it be possible, let this cup pass from me.' [Matthew 26:39.] He had wrestled with the superincumbent load in the wilderness, He had struggled against the powers of darkness that had been let loose upon Him there; placed below all things, His mind surcharged with agony and pain, lonely and apparently helpless and forsaken, in His agony the blood oozed from His pores. Thus rejected by His own, attacked by the powers of darkness, and seemingly forsaken by His God, on the cross He bowed beneath the accumulated load, and cried out in anguish, 'My God, my God, why hast thou forsaken me?' [Matthew 27:46; Mark 15:34.] When death approached to relieve Him from His horrible position, a ray of hope appeared through the abyss of darkness with which He had been surrounded, and in a spasm of relief, seeing the bright future beyond, He said, 'It is finished! Father, into thy hands I commend my spirit.' [John 19:30; Luke 23:46.] As a God, He descended below all things, and made Himself subject to man in man's fallen condition; as a man, He grappled with all the circumstances incident to His sufferings in the world. Anointed, indeed, with the oil of gladness above His fellows, He struggled with and overcame the powers of men and devils, of earth and hell combined; and aided by this superior power of the Godhead, He vanquished death, hell and the grave, and arose triumphant as the Son of God, the very eternal Father, the Messiah, the Prince of peace, the Redeemer, the Savior of the world; having finished and completed the work pertaining to the atonement, which His Father had given Him to do as the Son of God and the Son of Man. As the Son of Man, He endured all that it was possible for flesh and blood to endure; as the Son of God He triumphed over all, and forever ascended to the right hand of God, to further carry out the designs of Jehovah pertaining to the world and to the human family.

" . . . His suffering affected universal nature. . . . When He gave up the ghost, the solid rocks were riven, the foundations of the earth trembled, earthquakes shook the continents and rent the isles of the sea, a deep darkness overspread the sky, the mighty waters overflowed their accustomed bounds, huge mountains sank and valleys rose, the handiwork of feeble men was overthrown, their cities were engulfed or consumed by the vivid shafts of lightning, and all material things were convulsed with the throes of seeming dissolution."[7]

The mission of Jesus Christ includes the Atonement, which is the power whereby the two deaths—temporal (or physical) and spiritual—are overcome.

Without Christ, Satan would reign supreme: "O the wisdom of God, his mercy and grace! For behold, if the flesh should rise no more our spirits must become subject to that angel who fell from before the presence of the Eternal God, and became the devil, to rise no more.

"And our spirits must have become like unto him, and we become devils, angels to a devil, to be shut out from the presence of our God, and to remain with the father of lies, in misery, like unto himself; yea, to that being who beguiled our first parents, who transformeth himself nigh unto an angel of light, and stirreth up the children of men unto secret combinations of murder and all manner of secret works of darkness.

"O how great the goodness of our God, who prepareth a way for our escape from the grasp of this awful monster; yea, that monster, death and hell, which I call the death of the body, and also the death of the spirit" (2 Nephi 9:8–10).

Satan cannot keep in permanent bondage those who have suffered a physical death because Christ has provided a universal resurrection for all mankind: "And because of the way of deliverance of our God, the Holy One of Israel, this death, of which I have spoken, which is the temporal, shall deliver up its dead; which death is the grave" (2 Nephi 9:11).

Satan tries to keep the children of God in a state of spiritual death. He boasts of the expulsion of Adam and Eve from God's presence in the Garden of Eden, and has tried ever since to prevent God's children from communicating with their Father. Satan desires that we not recognize sin as being bad. He teaches that repentance is not necessary because there is no sin. He wants God's children to remain spiritually dead. He does not want them to be clean and

70

pure, or to qualify to return to God. He does not want them to follow the teachings and precepts of God on earth as taught by The
Church of Jesus Christ of Latter-day Saints.

"And this death of which I have spoken, which is the spiritual
death, shall deliver up its dead; which spiritual death is hell; wherefore, death and hell must deliver up their dead, and hell must
deliver up its captive spirits, and the grave must deliver up its captive bodies, and the bodies and the spirits of men will be restored
one to the other; and it is by the power of the resurrection of the
Holy One of Israel.

"O how great the plan of our God! For on the other hand, the
paradise of God must deliver up the spirits of the righteous, and the
grave deliver up the body of the righteous; and the spirit and the
body is restored to itself again, and all men become incorruptible,
and immortal, and they are living souls, having a perfect knowledge
like unto us in the flesh, save it be that our knowledge shall be perfect.

"Wherefore, we shall have a perfect knowledge of all our guilt,
and our uncleanness, and our nakedness; and the righteous shall
have a perfect knowledge of their enjoyment, and their righteousness, being clothed with purity, yea, even with the robe of righteousness.

"And it shall come to pass that when all men shall have passed
from this first death unto life, insomuch as they have become
immortal, they must appear before the judgment-seat of the Holy
One of Israel; and then cometh the judgment, and then must they
be judged according to the holy judgment of God.

"And assuredly, as the Lord liveth, for the Lord God hath spoken it, and it is his eternal word, which cannot pass away, that they
who are righteous shall be righteous still, and they who are filthy
shall be filthy still; wherefore, they who are filthy are the devil and

his angels; and they shall go away into everlasting fire, prepared for them; and their torment is as a lake of fire and brimstone, whose flame ascendeth up forever and ever and has no end.

"O the greatness and the justice of our God! For he executeth all his words, and they have gone forth out of his mouth, and his law must be fulfilled. But, behold, the righteous, the saints of the Holy One of Israel, they who have believed in the Holy One of Israel, they who have endured the crosses of the world, and despised the shame of it, they shall inherit the kingdom of God, which was prepared for them from the foundation of the world, and their joy shall be full forever.

"O the greatness of the mercy of our God, the Holy One of Israel! For he delivereth his saints from that awful monster the devil, and death, and hell, and that lake of fire and brimstone, which is endless torment.

"O how great the holiness of our God! For he knoweth all things, and there is not anything save he knows it. And he cometh into the world that he may save all men if they will hearken unto his voice; for behold, he suffereth the pains of all men, yea, the pains of every living creature, both men, women, and children, who belong to the family of Adam.

"And he suffereth this that the resurrection might pass upon all men, that all might stand before him at the great and judgment day. And he commandeth all men that they must repent, and be baptized in his name, having perfect faith in the Holy One of Israel, or they cannot be saved in the kingdom of God.

"And if they will not repent and believe in his name, and be baptized in his name, and endure to the end, they must be damned; for the Lord God, the Holy One of Israel, has spoken it" (2 Nephi 9:12–24).

The greatness of the justice and mercy of God is integral to the

Atonement and the mission of Jesus Christ. These doctrines will be covered in a later chapter, but it suffices to say here that Christ has provided the mercy that satisfies the demands of justice through the principles and ordinances of his gospel, including repentance, baptism, and the sacrament.

"Wherefore, he has given a law; and where there is no law given there is no punishment; and where there is no punishment there is no condemnation; and where there is no condemnation the mercies of the Holy One of Israel have claim upon them, because of the atonement; for they are delivered by the power of him.

"For the atonement satisfieth the demands of his justice upon all those who have not the law given to them, that they are delivered from that awful monster, death and hell, and the devil, and the lake of fire and brimstone, which is endless torment; and they are restored to that God who gave them breath, which is the Holy One of Israel.

"But wo unto him that has the law given, yea, that has all the commandments of God, like unto us, and that transgresseth them, and that wasteth the days of his probation, for awful is his state!" (2 Nephi 9:25–27).

About sixty-five years before Christ appeared to the Nephites, Helaman counseled his sons Lehi and Nephi to remember the words of King Benjamin and Amulek: "O remember, remember, my sons, the words which king Benjamin spake unto his people; yea, remember that there is no other way nor means whereby man can be saved, only through the atoning blood of Jesus Christ, who shall come; yea, remember that he cometh to redeem the world.

"And remember also the words which Amulek spake unto Zeezrom, in the city of Ammonihah; for he said unto him that the Lord surely should come to redeem his people, but that he should not come to redeem them in their sins, but to redeem them from their sins.

"And he hath power given unto him from the Father to redeem them from their sins because of repentance; therefore he hath sent his angels to declare the tidings of the conditions of repentance, which bringeth unto the power of the Redeemer, unto the salvation of their souls" (Helaman 5:9–11).

When Christ appeared to the Nephites, he testified of his divine and holy mission: "Behold, I am Jesus Christ, whom the prophets testified shall come into the world. And behold, I am the light and the life of the world; and I have drunk out of that bitter cup which the Father hath given me, and have glorified the Father in taking upon me the sins of the world, in the which I have suffered the will of the Father in all things from the beginning.

"And it came to pass that when Jesus had spoken these words the whole multitude fell to the earth; for they remembered that it had been prophesied among them that Christ should show himself unto them after his ascension into heaven.

"And it came to pass that the Lord spake unto them saying: Arise and come forth unto me, that ye may thrust your hands into my side, and also that ye may feel the prints of the nails in my hands and in my feet, that ye may know that I am the God of Israel, and the God of the whole earth, and have been slain for the sins of the world.

"And it came to pass that the multitude went forth, and thrust their hands into his side, and did feel the prints of the nails in his hands and in his feet; and this they did do, going forth one by one until they had all gone forth, and did see with their eyes and did feel with their hands, and did know of a surety and did bear record, that it was he, of whom it was written by the prophets, that should come.

"And when they had all gone forth and had witnessed for themselves, they did cry out with one accord, saying: Hosanna! Blessed be the name of the Most High God! And they did fall down at the feet of Jesus, and did worship him" (3 Nephi 11:10–17).

Christ testified that he had been "slain for the sins of the world" (3 Nephi 11:14). He gave evidence of his crucifixion by allowing the people to "thrust their hands into his side, and . . . feel the prints of the nails in his hands and in his feet" (3 Nephi 11:15).

In modern-day revelation, Jesus Christ has reaffirmed his mission as the Savior of all mankind: "For behold, I, God, have suffered these things for all, that they might not suffer if they would repent; but if they would not repent they must suffer even as I; which suffering caused myself, even God, the greatest of all, to tremble because of pain, and to bleed at every pore, and to suffer both body and spirit—and would that I might not drink the bitter cup, and shrink—nevertheless, glory be to the Father, and I partook and finished my preparations unto the children of men" (D&C 19:16–19).

Oh, the marvelous beauty of the mission of Jesus Christ. How great and wonderful are his works! Can we, as mere mortals, ever truly appreciate what he has done for us? Can we show our love and thanksgiving for Christ's life and sacrifice by striving harder to keep his commandments?

Notes

1. *Merriam-Webster's Collegiate Dictionary* (Springfield, Massachusetts: Merriam-Webster, 1999), 999.

2. *Merriam-Webster's Collegiate Dictionary*, 979.

3. John Taylor, *The Mediation and Atonement* (Salt Lake City: Deseret News, 1882), 132–33.

4. Bruce R. McConkie, *The Mortal Messiah: From Bethlehem to Calvary*, 4 vols. (Salt Lake City: Deseret Book, 1981), 4:124–25.

5. Frederic W. Farrar, *The Life of Christ* (Salt Lake City: Bookcraft, 1994), 575–77.

6. McConkie, *Mortal Messiah*, 4:126–27.

7. Taylor, *Mediation and Atonement*, 150–52.

VI
THE SAVIOR'S SPECIAL ATTRIBUTES

Who was Jesus? Who was his mother, Mary, and what special attributes did she give her son that made the Atonement possible? What special powers and attributes did Christ inherit from his Father? What was it about the Savior's life that gave him power to work out the Atonement?

What can we learn from Christ's sinless life that will help us prepare to return to our Heavenly Father? Can we possibly understand what it meant for Christ to leave his home in the heavens and become subject to the physical, temporal laws of this earth, a sphere he had created?

The birth of Jesus in Bethlehem is one of the best-known events in all the world. The celebration of this scripturally predicted and recorded event is acknowledged each year at Christmas time in Christian countries around the world, just as his death and resurrection are remembered during Easter.

Jesus Christ is the only person ever born on earth who could atone for the sins of mankind. "Now there is not any man that can sacrifice his own blood which will atone for the sins of another" (Alma 34:11). Only Christ could lay down his life in sacrifice for man's sins. "For it is expedient that there should be a great and last sacrifice; yea, not a sacrifice of man, neither of beast, neither of any manner of fowl; for it shall not be a human sacrifice; but it must be an infinite and eternal sacrifice" (Alma 34:10).

All of the sacrifices under the law of Moses were of no eternal consequence in the Atonement (see chapter 3). Only Christ's sacrifice could bring about the Atonement. Only Christ, with his special and unique characteristics, was able to satisfy the Father's requirement as the atoning and sacrificial lamb.

"Wherefore, redemption cometh in and through the Holy Messiah; for he is full of grace and truth. Behold, he offereth himself a sacrifice for sin, to answer the ends of the law, unto all those who have a broken heart and a contrite spirit; and unto none else can the ends of the law be answered" (2 Nephi 2:6–7).

Our understanding and comprehension of the Atonement is more complete as we understand and know Jesus Christ. Elder James E. Talmage wrote: "Simple as is the plan of redemption in its general features, it is confessedly a mystery in detail to the finite mind. President John Taylor has written in this wise: 'In some mysterious, incomprehensible way, Jesus assumed the responsibility which naturally would have devolved upon Adam; but which could only be accomplished through the mediation of Himself, and by taking upon Himself their sorrows, assuming their responsibilities, and bearing their transgressions or sins. In a manner to us incomprehensible and inexplicable, He bore the weight of the sins of the whole world, not only of Adam, but of his posterity; and in doing that, opened the kingdom of heaven, not only to all believers and all who obeyed the law of God, but to more than one-half of the human family who die before they come to years of maturity, as well as to the heathen, who, having died without law, will through His mediation be resurrected without law, and be judged without law, and thus participate, according to their capacity, works, and worth, in the blessings of His atonement.' (John Taylor, *Mediation and Atonement*, pp. 148, 149.)

"However incomplete may be our comprehension of the scheme of redemption through Christ's vicarious sacrifice in all its parts, we cannot reject it without becoming infidel; for it stands as the fundamental doctrine of all scripture, the very essence of the spirit of prophecy and revelation, the most prominent of all the declarations of God unto man."[1]

THE ATTRIBUTES OF CHRIST

Christ was the literal son of God the Father in both spirit and body. He was also the Only Begotten in the flesh. Mary was his mother in the flesh. Joseph, the noble husband of Mary, was the earthly tutor of Jesus during his formative years on earth.

Nephi's vision of the tree of life helps us understand the relationship of Christ to God the Father and to Mary, his mother: "And it came to pass that I saw the heavens open; and an angel came down and stood before me; and he said unto me: Nephi, what beholdest thou? And I said unto him: A virgin, most beautiful and fair above all other virgins.

"And he said unto me: Knowest thou the condescension of God? And I said unto him: I know that he loveth his children; nevertheless, I do not know the meaning of all things. And he said unto me: Behold, the virgin whom thou seest is the mother of the Son of God, after the manner of the flesh.

"And it came to pass that I beheld that she was carried away in the Spirit; and after she had been carried away in the Spirit for the space of a time the angel spake unto me, saying: Look! And I looked and beheld the virgin again, bearing a child in her arms. And the angel said unto me: Behold the Lamb of God, yea, even the Son of the Eternal Father!" (1 Nephi 11:14–21).

Elder Bruce R. McConkie gave further light and understanding: "Thus, God, an immortal man, was his Father; and Mary, a mortal woman, was his mother. He was begotten; he was conceived; he was born. From his immortal Father he inherited the power of immortality, which is the power to live; from his mortal mother he inherited the power of mortality, which is the power to die; and being thus dual in nature, being able to choose life or death, according to the will of the Father, he was able to work out the infinite and eternal atonement. Having chosen to die, as he did because he had the power of mortality, he could choose to live again because he had the power of immortality.

"This, then, is the doctrine of the divine Sonship. It took our Lord's mortal and his immortal powers to work out the atonement, for that supreme sacrifice required both death and resurrection. There is no salvation without death, even as there is no salvation without resurrection."[2]

President John Taylor noted the many unique attributes Jesus Christ inherited from his Father: "The Father gave Him power to have life in Himself: 'For as the Father hath life in himself, so hath he given to the Son to have life in himself' [John 5:26]; and further, He had power, when all mankind had lost their life, to restore life to them again; and hence He is the Resurrection and the Life, which power no other man possesses.

"Another distinction is, that having this life in Himself, He had power, as He said, to lay down His life and to take it up again, which power was also given Him by the Father. This is also a power which no other being associated with this earth possesses.

"Again, He is the brightness of His Father's glory and the

express image of His person. Also, He doeth what He seeth the Father do, while we only do that which we are permitted and empowered to do by Him.

"He is the Elect, the Chosen, and one of the Presidency in the heavens, and in Him dwells all the fulness of the Godhead bodily, which could not be said of us in any of these particulars.

"Another thing is, that all power is given to Him in heaven and upon earth, which no earthly being could say. . . .

"He, in the nearness of His relationship to the Father, seems to occupy a position that no other person occupies. He is spoken of as His well beloved Son, as the Only Begotten of the Father—does not this mean the only begotten after the flesh? If He was the first born and obedient to the laws of His Father, did He not inherit the position by right to be the representative of God, the Savior and Redeemer of the world? And was it not His peculiar right and privilege as the firstborn, the legitimate heir of God, the Eternal Father, to step forth, accomplish and carry out the designs of His Heavenly Father pertaining to the redemption, salvation and exaltation of man? And being Himself without sin (which no other mortal was), He took the position of Savior and Redeemer, which by right belonged to Him as the first born. And does it not seem that in having a body specially prepared, and being the offspring of God, both in body and spirit, He stood preeminently in the position of the Son of God, or in the place of God, and was God, and was thus the fit and only personage capable of making an infinite atonement?"[3]

Christ spoke of his unique character as he prayed to his Father: "As thou hast given him power over all flesh, that he should give eternal life to as many as thou hast given him. And this is life eternal, that they might know thee the only true God, and Jesus Christ, whom thou hast sent" (John 17:2–3).

CHRIST VOLUNTARILY GAVE HIS LIFE AS A SACRIFICE

As recorded in the book of John, Christ instructed his disciples on the divine nature of his being and mission. His death would be voluntary; no man would take his life from him.

"I am the good shepherd, and know my sheep, and am known of mine. As the Father knoweth me, even so know I the Father: and I lay down my life for the sheep.

"And other sheep I have, which are not of this fold: them also I must bring, and they shall hear my voice; and there shall be one fold, and one shepherd.

"Therefore doth my Father love me, because I lay down my life, that I might take it again. No man taketh it from me, but I lay it down of myself. I have power to lay it down, and I have power to take it again. This commandment have I received of my Father" (John 10:14–18).

As he hung on the cross, near the ninth hour, having been nailed to the cross on the third hour, Christ voluntarily "yielded up the ghost."

"And about the ninth hour Jesus cried with a loud voice, saying, Eli, Eli, lama sabachthani? that is to say, My God, my God, why hast thou forsaken me?

"Some of them that stood there, when they heard that, said, This man calleth for Elias. And straightway one of them ran, and took a spunge, and filled it with vinegar, and put it on a reed, and gave him to drink. The rest said, Let be, let us see whether Elias will come to save him.

"Jesus, when he had cried again with a loud voice, yielded up the ghost" (Matthew 27:46–50).

"After this, Jesus knowing that all things were now accomplished, that the scripture might be fulfilled, saith, I thirst. Now there was set a vessel full of vinegar: and they filled a spunge with vinegar, and put it upon hyssop, and put it to his mouth. When Jesus therefore had received the vinegar, he said, It is finished: and he bowed his head, and gave up the ghost" (John 19:28–30).

The voluntary offering of his life as an infinite and eternal sacrifice for all mankind was a fulfillment of the will of the Father. Christ explained this to the Nephites when he appeared to them following his Crucifixion.

"Behold I have given unto you my gospel, and this is the gospel which I have given unto you—that I came into the world to do the will of my Father, because my Father sent me. And my Father sent me that I might be lifted up upon the cross; and after that I had been lifted up upon the cross, that I might draw all men unto me, that as I have been lifted up by men even so should men be lifted up by the Father, to stand before me, to be judged of their works, whether they be good or whether they be evil" (3 Nephi 27:13–14).

Christ was absolutely obedient to the will of his Father, which helps us to more easily understand the voluntary nature of his atoning sacrifice.

CHRIST VOLUNTARILY SUFFERED FOR US

Seven hundred years before the birth of Christ, the great prophet Isaiah bore witness of his birth, life, death, and resurrection. The following passage of scripture is one of the most remarkable and accurate in minute detail of all of the Messianic scriptures of the Old Testament.

"Who hath believed our report? and to whom is the arm of the Lord revealed? For he shall grow up before him as a tender plant, and as a root out of a dry ground: he hath no form nor comeliness; and when we shall see him, there is no beauty that we should desire him.

"He is despised and rejected of men; a man of sorrows, and acquainted with grief: and we hid as it were our faces from him; he was despised, and we esteemed him not. Surely he hath borne our griefs, and carried our sorrows: yet we did esteem him stricken, smitten of God, and afflicted.

"But he was wounded for our transgressions, he was bruised for our iniquities: the chastisement of our peace was upon him; and with his stripes we are healed. All we like sheep have gone astray; we have turned every one to his own way; and the Lord hath laid on him the iniquity of us all.

"He was oppressed, and he was afflicted, yet he opened not his mouth: he is brought as a lamb to the slaughter, and as a sheep before her shearers is dumb, so he openeth not his mouth. He was taken from prison and from judgment: and who shall declare his generation? for he was cut off out of the land of the living: for the transgression of my people was he stricken.

"And he made his grave with the wicked, and with the rich in his death; because he had done no violence, neither was any deceit in his mouth. Yet it pleased the Lord to bruise him; he hath put him to grief: when thou shalt make his soul an offering for sin, he shall see his seed, he shall prolong his days, and the pleasure of the Lord shall prosper in his hand.

"He shall see of the travail of his soul, and shall be satisfied: by his knowledge shall my righteous servant justify many; for he shall bear their iniquities. Therefore will I divide him a portion with the great, and he shall divide the spoil with the strong; because he hath poured out his soul unto death: and he was numbered with the transgressors; and he bare the sin of many, and made intercession for the transgressors" (Isaiah 53:1–12).

In modern days, the Lord has revealed the depth of his suffering and sacrifice for us: "For behold, I, God, have suffered these things for all, that they might not suffer if they would repent; but if they would not repent they must suffer even as I; which suffering caused myself, even God, the greatest of all, to tremble because of pain, and to bleed at every pore, and to suffer both body and spirit—and would that I might not drink the bitter cup, and shrink—nevertheless, glory be to the Father, and I partook and finished my preparations unto the children of men" (D&C 19:16–19).

CHRIST SUFFERED ALONE

The uniqueness of the sole sacrifice of Jesus Christ is described in the Doctrine and Covenants and in the Book of Mormon: "And it shall be said: Who is this that cometh down from God in heaven with dyed garments; yea, from the regions which are not known, clothed in his glorious apparel, traveling in the greatness of his strength?

"And he shall say: I am he who spake in righteousness, mighty to save. And the Lord shall be red in his apparel, and his garments like him that treadeth in the wine-vat. And so great shall be the glory of his presence that the sun shall hide his face in shame, and the moon shall withhold its light, and the stars shall be hurled from their places.

"And his voice shall be heard: I have trodden the wine-press alone, and have brought judgment upon all people; and none were with me" (D&C 133:46–50).

"And he shall go forth, suffering pains and afflictions and temptations of every kind; and this that the word might be fulfilled which saith he will take upon him the pains and the sicknesses of his people" (Alma 7:11).

In a beautiful and moving analogy of the willingness of Abraham to sacrifice his only son, Isaac, Elder Melvin J. Ballard described the voluntary and solitary sacrifice of Jesus Christ in the following words:

"I think as I read the story of Abraham's sacrifice of his son Isaac that our Father is trying to tell us what it cost Him to give His Son as a gift to the world. You remember the story of how Abraham's son came after long years of waiting and was looked upon by his worthy sire, Abraham, as more precious than all his other possessions; yet, in the midst of his rejoicing, Abraham was told to take this only son and offer him as a sacrifice to the Lord. He responded. Can you feel what was in the heart of Abraham on that occasion? You love your son just as Abraham did; perhaps not quite so much, because of the peculiar circumstances, but what do you think was in his heart when he started away from Mother Sarah and they bade her goodbye? What do you think was in his heart when he saw Isaac bidding farewell to his mother to take that three days' journey to the appointed place where the sacrifice was to be made? I imagine it was about all Father Abraham could do to keep from showing his great grief and sorrow at that parting, but he and his son trudged along three days toward the appointed place, Isaac carrying the fagots that were to consume the sacrifice. The two travelers rested, finally, at the mountainside, and the men who had accompanied them were told to remain while Abraham and his son started up the hill.

"The boy then said to his father: 'Why, Father, we have the fagots; we have the fire to burn the sacrifice; but where is the sacrifice?'

"It must have pierced the heart of Father Abraham to hear the trusting and confiding son say: 'You have forgotten the sacrifice.' Looking at the youth, his son of promise, the poor father could only say: 'The Lord will provide.'

"They ascended the mountain, gathered the stones together,

and placed the fagots upon them. Then Isaac was bound, hand and foot, kneeling upon the altar. I presume Abraham, like a true father, must have given his son his farewell kiss, his blessing, his love, and his soul must have been drawn out in that hour of agony toward his son who was to die by the hand of his own father. Every step proceeded until the cold steel was drawn and the hand raised that was to strike the blow to let out the life's blood, when the angel of the Lord said: 'It is enough.'

"Our Father in heaven went through all that and more, for in His case the hand was not stayed. He loved His Son, Jesus Christ, better than Abraham ever loved Isaac, for our Father had with Him His Son, our Redeemer, in the eternal worlds, faithful and true for ages, standing in a place of trust and honor, and the Father loved him so dearly, and yet He allowed this well-beloved Son to descend from His place of glory and honor, where millions did Him homage, down to the earth, a condescension that is not within the power of man to conceive. He came to receive the insult, the abuse, and the crown of thorns. God heard the cry of His Son in that moment of great grief and agony, in the garden when the pores of His body opened and drops of blood stood upon Him, and He cried out: 'Father, if thou be willing, remove this cup from me.'

"I ask you, what father and mother could stand by and listen to the cry of their children in distress, in this world, and not render assistance? I have heard of mothers throwing themselves into raging streams when they could not swim a stroke to save their drowning children, rushing into burning buildings to rescue those whom they loved.

"We cannot stand by and listen to those cries without its touching our hearts. The Lord has not given us the power to save our own. He has given us faith, and we submit to the inevitable, but He had the power to save, and He loved His Son, and He could have saved Him. He might have rescued Him from the insult of the crowds. He might have rescued Him when the crown of thorns was placed upon His head. He might have rescued Him when the Son, hanging between the two thieves, was mocked with, 'Save thyself, and come down from the cross. He saved others; himself he cannot save.' He listened to all this. He saw that Son condemned; He saw Him drag the cross through the streets of Jerusalem and faint under its load. He saw the Son finally upon Calvary; He saw His body stretched out upon the wooden cross; He saw the cruel nails driven through hands and feet, and the blows that broke the skin, tore the flesh, and let out the life's blood of His Son. He looked upon that.

"In the case of our Father, the knife was not stayed, but it fell, and the life's blood of His Beloved Son went out. His Father looked on with great grief and agony over His Beloved Son, until there seems to have come a moment when even our Saviour cried out in despair: 'My God, my God, why hast thou forsaken me?'

"In that hour I think I can see our dear Father behind the veil looking upon these dying struggles until even he could not endure it any longer; and, like the mother who bids farewell to her dying child and has to be taken out of the room so as not to look upon the last struggles, so He bowed His head and hid in some part of His universe, His great heart almost breaking for the love that He had for His Son. Oh, in that moment when He might have saved His Son, I thank Him and praise Him that He did not fail us, for He had not only the love of His son in mind, but He also had love for us. I rejoice that He did not interfere, and that His love for us made it possible for Him to endure to look upon the sufferings of His Son and give Him finally to us, our Saviour and our Redeemer. Without Him, without His sacrifice, we would have remained, and we would never have come glorified into His presence. And so this is what it cost, in part, for our Father in heaven to give the gift of His Son unto men."[4]

CHRIST WAS WITHOUT SIN

Only a man who is without sin could atone for the sins of another. Just as the lamb sacrificed under the Mosaic law was a lamb without blemish, so was Christ without sin.

"For he hath made him to be sin for us, who knew no sin; that we might be made the righteousness of God in him" (2 Corinthians 5:21). "For even hereunto were ye called: because Christ also suffered for us, leaving us an example, that ye should follow his steps: who did no sin, neither was guile found in his mouth" (1 Peter 2:21–22).

The Father was "well pleased" with the Son, who said, "Father, behold the sufferings and death of him who did no sin, in whom thou wast well pleased; behold the blood of thy Son which was shed, the blood of him whom thou gavest that thyself might be glorified" (D&C 45:4).

Only a man without sin could redeem all mankind from Adam till the great judgment day.

"O how great the holiness of our God! For he knoweth all things, and there is not anything save he knows it. And he cometh into the world that he may save all men if they will hearken unto his voice; for behold, he suffereth the pains of all men, yea, the pains of every living creature, both men, women, and children, who belong to the family of Adam.

"And he suffereth this that the resurrection might pass upon all men, that all might stand before him at the great and judgment day" (2 Nephi 9:20–22).

CHRIST IS OUR ADVOCATE AND MEDIATOR

An *advocate* is one who pleads the cause of another. A *mediator* is one who attempts to reconcile two parties, who acts as an intermediary agent in bringing, effecting, or communicating.

Elder McConkie explained these two terms: "According to the law of advocacy, our Lord intercedes for the faithful saints and pleads their cause in the courts above. 'He claimeth all those who have faith in him,' Mormon says, 'and they who have faith in him will cleave unto every good thing; wherefore he advocateth the cause of the children of men; and he dwelleth eternally in the heavens.' (Moroni 7:28.) 'If any man sin, we have an advocate with the Father,' John tells us, who is 'Jesus Christ the righteous.' (1 John 2:1.) And in a revelation to the Prophet Joseph Smith, the Lord Jesus said: 'Listen to him who is the advocate with the Father, who is pleading your cause before him—saying: Father, behold the sufferings and death of him who did no sin, in whom thou wast well pleased; behold the blood of thy Son which was shed, the blood of him whom thou gavest that thyself might be glorified; wherefore, Father, spare these my brethren that believe on my name, that they may come unto me and have everlasting life.' (D&C 45:3–5.)"⁵

Elder McConkie also wrote: "It was God our Father who made the law of mediation; he established it as one of the chief provisions of his eternal plan of salvation. He is the one who appointed his Only Begotten Son to stand as the Mediator between himself and fallen men. Christ is our Mediator; he intervenes between God and man to effect a reconciliation; he interposes himself between parties at variance. He who committed no sin invites his mortal brethren to forsake their sins and thus place themselves in harmony and unity with the Sinless Son and the Sinless Father.

"Jesus is called the Mediator of the new covenant, to distinguish him from Moses, the mediator of the old covenant. The blessings of the old covenant, of the old testament, of the law of carnal commandments, came to Israel through Moses; he was the great lawgiver who stood between the Lord and the people in administering to their needs. The blessings of the new covenant, of the new testament, of the everlasting gospel, come to all men through Jesus Christ. He is the Eternal Lawgiver who stands between God and all men; he invites men to cleanse themselves from sin and receive salvation with him in the kingdom of his Father. Thus it is written that 'the law was given through Moses, but life and truth came through Jesus Christ. For the law was after a carnal commandment, to the administration of death; but the gospel was after the power of an endless life, through Jesus Christ, the Only Begotten Son, who is in the bosom of the Father.' (JST, John 1:17–18.)"[6]

The concept of Christ being our advocate and mediator with the Father has biblical origins: "Their Redeemer is strong; the Lord of hosts is his name: he shall throughly plead their cause, that he may give rest to the land, and disquiet the inhabitants of Babylon" (Jeremiah 50:34).

"How much more shall the blood of Christ, who through the eternal Spirit offered himself without spot to God, purge your conscience from dead works to serve the living God? And for this cause he is the mediator of the new testament, that by means of death, for the redemption of the transgressions that were under the first testament, they which are called might receive the promise of eternal inheritance" (Hebrews 9:14–15).

Qualifying to enter the celestial kingdom of glory assumes recognition of the mediating role of Jesus Christ: "These are they who are just men made perfect through Jesus the mediator of the new covenant, who wrought out this perfect atonement through the shedding of his own blood" (D&C 76:69).

We recognize the Savior's mediating role when we conclude

our prayers "in the name of Jesus Christ." Christ is the one, the means, the person through whom we go to gain access to the Father. When we approach the Father through Jesus Christ—our advocate and mediator—the Savior intercedes on our behalf.

"According to the law of intercession, as ordained and established by the Father, the Lord Jesus has 'power to make intercession for the children of men.' (Mosiah 15:8.) That is to say, he has the role of interceding, of mediating, of praying, petitioning, and entreating the Father to grant mercy and blessings to men. One of Isaiah's great Messianic prophecies says: 'He bare the sins of many, and made intercession for the transgressors.' (Isaiah 53:12.) Of this ministry of intercession, Paul affirms: 'It is Christ that died, yea rather, that is risen again, who is even at the right hand of God, who also maketh intercession for us.' (Romans 8:34.) And it is Lehi who tells us: Christ 'is the firstfruits unto God, inasmuch as he shall make intercession for all the children of men; and they that believe in him shall be saved. And because of the intercession for all, all men come unto God; wherefore, they stand in the presence of him, to be judged of him according to the truth and holiness which is in him.' (2 Nephi 2:9–10.)"[7]

THE CONDESCENSION OF GOD

One of the greatest of all the attributes of Jesus Christ, which uniquely qualify him to be the Redeemer and Savior of all mankind, is found in an understanding of the condescension of God. In Nephi's vision of the tree of life, which was an explanation of Lehi's dream, we find the following:

"And it came to pass that I saw the heavens open; and an angel came down and stood before me; and he said unto me: Nephi, what beholdest thou? And I said unto him: A virgin, most beautiful and fair above all other virgins. And he said unto me: Knowest thou the condescension of God? . . . And the angel said unto me again: Look and behold the condescension of God!

"And I looked and beheld the Redeemer of the world, of whom my father had spoken; and I also beheld the prophet who should prepare the way before him. And the Lamb of God went forth and was baptized of him; and after he was baptized, I beheld the heavens open, and the Holy Ghost come down out of heaven and abide upon him in the form of a dove.

"And I beheld that he went forth ministering unto the people, in power and great glory; and the multitudes were gathered together to hear him; and I beheld that they cast him out from among them. . . . And it came to pass that the angel spake unto me again, saying: Look! And I looked and beheld the Lamb of God, that he was taken by the people; yea, the Son of the everlasting God was judged of the world; and I saw and bear record.

"And I, Nephi, saw that he was lifted up upon the cross and slain for the sins of the world. And after he was slain I saw the multitudes of the earth, that they were gathered together to fight against the apostles of the Lamb; for thus were the twelve called by the angel of the Lord" (1 Nephi 11:14–16, 26–28, 32–34).

In witnessing the life of Christ and his birth, baptism, ministry, Crucifixion, death, and Resurrection, Nephi and Lehi saw "the condescension of God." The dictionary defines *condescension* as a "voluntary descent from one's rank or dignity in relations with an inferior."[8]

Elder McConkie offered this definition: "For Christ to be the Son of God means that God was his Father in the literal and true sense of the word; for our Lord to be the Only Begotten in the flesh means that he was begotten by God, who is a Holy Man. 'The condescension of God,' of which the scriptures speak, means that the Immortal Father—the glorified, exalted, enthroned ruler of the

93

universe—came down from his station of dominion and power to become the Father of a Son who would be born of Mary, 'after the manner of the flesh.' (1 Nephi 11:16–18.)"[9]

Robert L. Millet said it this way: "The condescension of God the Son thus consists in the fact that the Eternal One would 'descend from his throne divine,' be born in the most humble circumstances, become among the most helpless of all creation—a human infant—and submit to the refining influences of mortal life."[10]

Visualize the role of Christ with the Father as the creator of "worlds without number" (Moses 1:33). All things in the world are subject to Christ, yet he was willing to come down from the Father and live upon one of the worlds he had helped create.

"And now Abinadi said unto them: I would that ye should understand that God himself shall come down among the children of men, and shall redeem his people. And because he dwelleth in flesh he shall be called the Son of God, and having subjected the flesh to the will of the Father, being the Father and the Son—

"The Father, because he was conceived by the power of God; and the Son, because of the flesh; thus becoming the Father and Son—and they are one God, yea, the very Eternal Father of heaven and of earth.

"And thus the flesh becoming subject to the Spirit, or the Son to the Father, being one God, suffereth temptation, and yieldeth not to the temptation, but suffereth himself to be mocked, and scourged, and cast out, and disowned by his people. . . .

"Yea, even so he shall be led, crucified, and slain, the flesh becoming subject even unto death, the will of the Son being swallowed up in the will of the Father" (Mosiah 15:1–5, 7).

What can we understand from the condescension of God?

Bishop Richard C. Edgley beautifully described Christ's condescension in a presentation to the Quorums of the Seventy:

"He descended to be born of a mortal woman. He descended to be baptized of man, even though He was perfect and sinless. He descended to minister to the humblest of the humble. He descended to subject Himself to the will of the Father, suffering Himself to be tempted, mocked, scourged, cast out and disowned, even though he was all powerful. He descended to be judged of the world, even though He was the judge of the world. He descended to be lifted up on the cross and slain for the sins of the world, even though no man could take away His life.

"Like the vastness of God's creations, incomprehensible and infinite, His suffering is equally incomprehensible, as His atonement is also infinite. His condescension is an integral, necessary, and inseparable part of the atonement. The atonement itself was predicated upon His willingness to descend and suffer. His condescension, as part of the atonement, is probably as essential to the redemption of mankind as the garden or the cross. It is His free gift to all mankind—a gift that could be obtained no other way. It resulted from His willingness to descend. He descended not because of obligation, nor for glory, but only for love. His condescension to redeem us was the price He paid to provide free salvation and exaltation. As the song rolls on, 'I scarce can take it in.'

"It is interesting to note that it is at the extremity of His suffering, His greatest condescension, that we witness the majesty of His mission. It was at this time, His greatest humiliation and lowest state, that He gave greatest glory to His Father in Heaven and then signaled the completion of His mission by simply uttering the words, 'It is finished.' Indeed, He had descended to fulfill His Father's will."[11]

President John Taylor has explained: "In the economy of God pertaining to the salvation of the human family, we are told in the scriptures that it was necessary that Christ should descend below all things, that He might be raised above all things."[12]

"He that ascended up on high, as also he descended below all things, in that he comprehended all things, that he might be in all and through all things, the light of truth" (D&C 88:6).

President John Taylor continues: "It was further necessary that He should descend below all things, in order that He might raise others above all things; for if He could not raise Himself and be exalted through those principles brought about by the atonement, He could not raise others; He could not do for others what He could not do for Himself, and hence it was necessary for Him to descend below all things that He might be raised above all things, that by and through the same power that He obtained His exaltation, they also, through His atonement, expiation and intercession, might be raised to the same power with Him."[13]

To more fully appreciate and understand the Atonement of Jesus Christ, we must know the Savior. We must recognize his attributes and character. As Jesus taught in the great intercessory prayer, we must come to know him and the Father: "And this is life eternal, that they might know thee the only true God, and Jesus Christ, whom thou hast sent" (John 17:3).

NOTES

1. James E. Talmage, *The Articles of Faith* (Salt Lake City: Deseret Book, 1984), 69–70.

2. Bruce R. McConkie, *A New Witness for the Articles of Faith* (Salt Lake City: Deseret Book, 1985), 111.

3. John Taylor, *The Mediation and Atonement* (Salt Lake City: Deseret News, 1882), 135–37.

4. Melvin R. Ballard, *Melvin J. Ballard—Crusader for Righteousness* (Salt Lake City: Bookcraft, 1966), 135–37.

5. McConkie, *New Witness*, 126.

6. McConkie, *New Witness*, 124–26.

7. McConkie, *New Witness*, 125–26.

8. *Merriam-Webster's Collegiate Dictionary* (Springfield, Massachusetts: Merriam-Webster, 1999), 240.

9. McConkie, *New Witness*, 111.

10. Robert L. Millet, "Another Testament of Jesus Christ," in *The Book of Mormon: First Nephi, The Doctrinal Foundation—Papers from the Second Annual Book of Mormon Symposium*, eds. Monte S. Nyman and Charles D. Tate Jr. (Provo, Utah: Brigham Young University Religious Studies Center, 1988), 169.

11. Richard C. Edgley, presentation to the Quorums of the Seventy, 20 March 1997.

12. Taylor, *Mediation and Atonement*, 144–45.

13. Taylor, *Mediation and Atonement*, 144–45.

VII
HOW THE ATONEMENT
WORKS IN OUR LIVES

Our challenge is to apply in our lives the steps necessary to allow us to enjoy the full blessings of the Atonement. The conditional aspects of the Atonement must be more than theories or principles without individual application. As we come to understand the Atonement, we must internalize in our individual lives the necessary traits, habits, and actions that will allow us to be worthy to experience fully the blessings of the Atonement.

Faith in the Lord Jesus Christ and true and complete repentance for all wrongdoings become our eternal quest. In addition, we must take upon ourselves sacred covenants by entering into holy ordinances.

As members of The Church of Jesus Christ of Latter-day Saints, we have greater access to truth and saving principles than other Christians. Therefore, we know that we will have to pay a penalty if we do not repent of our sins. As we examine our individual responsibility to live worthily of enjoying more fully the promises of the

Atonement, we gain a greater love for the Savior and a greater appreciation for his earthly mission to ransom us from our sins.

President Gordon B. Hinckley stated, "I sense in a measure the meaning of his atonement. I cannot comprehend it all. It is so vast in its reach and yet so intimate in its effect that it defies comprehension."[1]

KEY POINTS OF THE ATONEMENT

The Atonement may defy comprehension, but we can obtain an understanding of its simplicity and application in our lives if we diligently seek to acquire saving truth and knowledge. A simple explanation of the Atonement might contain the following key points:

1. There is a God and he has a Son, Jesus Christ.

2. The Father and the Son are perfect. They live in heaven, and they possess glorified bodies of spirit, flesh, and bones.

3. We have been placed on earth to acquire a physical body, gain experience, and prove ourselves worthy to return to our Heavenly Father.

4. Laws govern our physical life on earth and our privilege of returning to our Heavenly Father.

5. We sin when we transgress the law.

6. Sin requires us to be subject to a penalty or a punishment. This is an example of the law of justice.

7. Once we have sinned, we are unclean. Unless we have faith in Jesus Christ, repent, and take upon ourselves sacred covenants and ordinances, including baptism and the gift of the Holy Ghost by the laying on of hands, we cannot return to live with our Heavenly Father and his Son, Jesus Christ. No unclean thing can dwell in their presence. They are clean and we, if unrepentant, are unclean.

8. God has provided a means whereby we can overcome our sins and become clean by exercising faith in Jesus Christ and repenting of our sins and transgressions. This is possible because of the eternal law of mercy.

9. When we truly repent and fulfill certain principles and ordinances, our repentance satisfies the law of justice. If we do not repent, we are subject to the law of justice.

10. The one who implemented the plan on this earth whereby we can repent of our sins and qualify for the law of mercy to satisfy justice is Jesus Christ. The payment by Jesus Christ for everyone's sins is made possible by the law of mercy and is accomplished on this earth by his Atonement.

11. The name of this plan is the plan of redemption, the plan of salvation, or God's great plan of happiness.

12. The means by which the plan is fulfilled is the Atonement.

13. Jesus Christ wrought the Atonement by his condescension to come to this earth, be born of a mortal mother, be tempted and overcome all temptation, keep all the commandments, establish his Church and kingdom on earth, bow down in Gethsemane and take upon him the sins of all mankind, suffer pain beyond our ability to comprehend, and allow himself to be crucified upon a cross and suffer the most painful and horrendous of all deaths in order to provide the Resurrection for all mankind. He also provided the opportunity for all to be cleansed from sin.

14. Participation in the Atonement of Jesus Christ, which will permit us to repent of our sins and benefit from the law of mercy, is up to us. We can choose to qualify or we can choose not to qualify. We have our agency.

15. If we choose not to repent, we have no assurance that, upon our being resurrected, we will return to our Heavenly Father. As the

scriptures say, we will not return if we are not clean or sanctified (3 Nephi 27:19–20).

16. Resurrection from the dead, another part of the Atonement, is universal and applies to the entire human family.

17. The resurrection results in the reuniting of our physical bodies to our spirits following their separation at our physical death.

18. To be resurrected does not necessarily mean we will live with our Heavenly Father and his Son, Jesus Christ. If we have not repented, we will be resurrected with the same spirit and uncleanness we had at the time of our physical death.

19. The Atonement is applicable to all who have lived without a knowledge of the law or who are innocent before the law.

20. In the postmortal world the true gospel of Jesus Christ will be taught to those who knew not the law or did not repent while living as mortals on earth.

21. Necessary and sacred ordinances are performed on earth under the direction of those who hold the keys of sacred priesthood power for those who died without a knowledge of the law or who did not repent.

22. Acceptance of gospel principles that will result in the blessings of the Atonement is the responsibility of all God's children, whether they are taught and accept the principles during earth life or postmortal life.

23. Little children under the age of accountability and those who do not understand the law because of mental incapacity, are saved by the grace of Jesus Christ. Earthly ordinances need not be performed for them.

24. The great plan of happiness was established by and ordained of God.

25. We may reap the blessings and benefits of the Atonement in our lives because of Jesus Christ and through our obedience.

"For God so loved the world, that he gave his only begotten Son, that whosoever believeth in him should not perish, but have everlasting life. For God sent not his Son into the world to condemn the world; but that the world through him might be saved" (John 3:16–17).

CHRIST IS THE AUTHOR

Christ is the key. He is the one who made the plan active on this earth. Years ago, Charles W. Penrose, an apostle and counselor to President Heber J. Grant, wrote a series of pamphlets titled "Rays of Living Light," which were used by missionaries. Pamphlet number 3, titled "The Atonement—First Principles of the Gospel," contained the following statements:

"Christ gave himself a sacrifice to save mankind from their sins, not in their sins. His work is to redeem humanity by lifting it up to Deity. His Gospel teaches purification from sin and exaltation into the righteousness of God. The Atonement wrought out on Calvary is as much misunderstood by modern divines who preach it, as were the teachings of Moses and the Prophets by the sectaries who rejected the Nazarene. That Atonement was for a dual purpose. First, to redeem mankind from the consequences of the original sin committed in the Garden of Eden, and second, to open the way of salvation from the actual sins committed by the posterity of Adam.

"As to the first, redemption will come to all the race without effort on their part. Death came into the world in the beginning because the divine law was broken. It passed upon all the descendants of the transgressor. Christ gave himself a sacrifice for that sin. As by one came death, so by one will come life. 'As in Adam all die, even so in Christ shall all be made alive.' (1 Cor. 15:22). As the sons and daughters of Adam were not personally engaged in or responsible for the transgression which brought death, so they are not required to do anything in the work which shall restore them to life. The resurrection will be as broad as the death. The raising up will be co-extensive with the effects of the fall. But when through Christ the resurrection is accomplished, the dead, small and great, who are thus brought up and redeemed from the grave will be judged according to their works. (Rev. 20).

"As to the second—the actual sins of each individual, salvation will come through faith in Christ and obedience to his Gospel. Each intelligent person is accountable for his own acts. He must do what is required in order that he may be saved from his sins. The power is inherent in man to do right or to do wrong. In this he is a free agent. He can resist evil and do good, or resist good and do evil, as he elects. No matter how great may be the force of circumstances and environments, and the pressure of hereditary influences, the volition of the creature remains. The doctrine of rewards and punishments is predicated upon individual freedom of the will and personal responsibility for its exercise. Christ has done for mankind that and that alone which they were not able to do for themselves. That which they can perform is required of every one. They can believe, they can repent, and they can receive and obey the commandments of Christ given as conditions to salvation. Unless they do this, although they will be raised from the dead and appear before the Eternal Judge, they cannot be exalted to dwell in His presence.

"Thus it will be seen that while Christ died, unconditionally, for the original sin by which death came into the world, he died as a propitiation for the actual sins of the world conditionally."[2]

President Wilford Woodruff gave similar counsel and instruction: "The Savior came and tabernacled in the flesh, and entered upon the duties of the priesthood at thirty years of age. After laboring three and a half years he was crucified and put to death in fulfilment of certain predictions concerning him. He laid down his life as a sacrifice for sin, to redeem the world. When men are called upon to repent of their sins, the call has reference to their own individual sins, not to Adam's transgressions. What is called the original sin was atoned for through the death of Christ irrespective of any action on the part of man; also man's individual sin was atoned for by the same sacrifice, but on condition of his obedience to the gospel plan of salvation when proclaimed in his hearing."[3]

We should understand that redemption from the consequences of original sin is resurrection, the overcoming of physical death. This is the reuniting, eternally, of the body and the spirit. Every soul will experience this blessing. It is a gift from Jesus Christ. The only qualification we must pass to inherit this gift is to be born. Death will follow and resurrection will come thereafter.

The other redemption, that from the individual sins we commit, is not free. It is available through the principles and ordinances of the gospel of Jesus Christ and through individual obedience. "We believe that through the Atonement of Christ, all mankind may be saved, by obedience to the laws and ordinances of the gospel" (Articles of Faith 1:3).

The scriptures, especially the Book of Mormon, provide clear and explicit testimony of these truths: "Wherefore, redemption cometh in and through the Holy Messiah; for he is full of grace and truth. Behold, he offereth himself a sacrifice for sin, to answer the ends of the law, unto all those who have a broken heart and a contrite spirit; and unto none else can the ends of the law be answered.

"Wherefore, how great the importance to make these things known unto the inhabitants of the earth, that they may know that there is no flesh that can dwell in the presence of God, save it be through the merits, and mercy, and grace of the Holy Messiah, who layeth down his life according to the flesh, and taketh it again by the power of the Spirit, that he may bring to pass the resurrection of the dead, being the first that should rise" (2 Nephi 2:6–8).

Because of Jesus Christ's perfect love, he paid for the sins of all mankind by shedding his blood, thus implementing the plan of redemption. That plan takes into consideration the opposition introduced into the world by the fall of Adam and Eve.

"For it must needs be, that there is an opposition in all things. If not so, my first-born in the wilderness, righteousness could not be brought to pass, neither wickedness, neither holiness nor misery, neither good nor bad. Wherefore, all things must needs be a compound in one; wherefore, if it should be one body it must needs remain as dead, having no life neither death, nor corruption nor incorruption, happiness nor misery, neither sense nor insensibility.

"Wherefore, it must needs have been created for a thing of naught; wherefore there would have been no purpose in the end of its creation. Wherefore, this thing must needs destroy the wisdom of God and his eternal purposes, and also the power, and the mercy, and the justice of God.

"And if ye shall say there is no law, ye shall also say there is no sin. If ye shall say there is no sin, ye shall also say there is no righteousness. And if there be no righteousness there be no happiness. And if there be no righteousness nor happiness there be no punishment nor misery. And if these things are not there is no God. And if there is no God we are not, neither the earth; for there could have been no creation of things, neither to act nor to be acted upon; wherefore, all things must have vanished away.

"And now, my sons, I speak unto you these things for your profit and learning; for there is a God, and he hath created all things, both the heavens and the earth, and all things that in them are, both things to act and things to be acted upon" (2 Nephi 2:11–14).

THE EFFECTS OF SIN

We all sin. Only Christ was perfect and sinless. To sin is to break the laws of God. Just as there are laws on earth governing our actions, there are eternal laws with eternal consequences. Because there are laws and agency, there will be sin and punishment. Happiness comes from not sinning, which is righteousness, or from sincere repentance.

We know when we sin, and our memory of sin becomes both a blessing and a condemnation. It becomes a blessing if we are prompted to repent. It becomes an eternal condemnation if we fail to repent before we depart this life.

"Wherefore, we shall have a perfect knowledge of all our guilt, and our uncleanness, and our nakedness; and the righteous shall have a perfect knowledge of their enjoyment, and their righteousness, being clothed with purity, yea, even with the robe of righteousness.

"And it shall come to pass that when all men shall have passed from this first death unto life, insomuch as they have become immortal, they must appear before the judgment-seat of the Holy One of Israel; and then cometh the judgment, and then must they be judged according to the holy judgment of God.

"And assuredly, as the Lord liveth, for the Lord God hath spoken it, and it is his eternal word, which cannot pass away, that they who are righteous shall be righteous still, and they who are filthy shall be filthy still; wherefore, they who are filthy are the devil and his angels; and they shall go away into everlasting fire, prepared for them; and their torment is as a lake of fire and brimstone, whose flame ascendeth up forever and ever and has no end" (2 Nephi 9:14–16).

ALMA 42—A COMPREHENSIVE STUDY OF THE ATONEMENT

Alma 42 is one of the more difficult scriptural passages to understand, yet it possesses great truth and knowledge on the Atonement. The sins of Corianton, though distressing to his father, Alma, resulted in this beautiful chapter wherein Alma attempted to correct and save his son by teaching him pure doctrine. Alma made it clear that Adam would have lived forever with no opportunity to repent if he had partaken of the tree of life in the Garden of Eden.

"Now behold, my son, I will explain this thing unto thee. For behold, after the Lord God sent our first parents forth from the garden of Eden, to till the ground, from whence they were taken—yea, he drew out the man, and he placed at the east end of the garden of Eden, cherubim, and a flaming sword which turned every way, to keep the tree of life—

"Now, we see that the man had become as God, knowing good and evil; and lest he should put forth his hand, and take also of the tree of life, and eat and live forever, the Lord God placed cherubim and the flaming sword, that he should not partake of the fruit—and thus we see, that there was a time granted unto man to repent, yea, a probationary time, a time to repent and serve God.

"For behold, if Adam had put forth his hand immediately, and partaken of the tree of life, he would have lived forever, according to the word of God, having no space for repentance; yea, and also the word of God would have been void, and the great plan of salvation would have been frustrated.

"But behold, it was appointed unto man to die—therefore, as they were cut off from the tree of life they should be cut off from the face of the earth—and man became lost forever, yea, they became fallen man. . . . Now behold, it was not expedient that man should be reclaimed from this temporal death, for that would destroy the great plan of happiness" (Alma 42:2–6, 8).

Alma taught clearly that there are two deaths—physical and spiritual: "And now, ye see by this that our first parents were cut off both temporally and spiritually from the presence of the Lord; and thus we see they became subjects to follow after their own will. . . .

"Therefore, as the soul could never die, and the fall had brought upon all mankind a spiritual death as well as a temporal, that is, they were cut off from the presence of the Lord, it was expedient that mankind should be reclaimed from this spiritual death" (Alma 42:7, 9).

Because of our disobedience, we can be reclaimed from our fallen state only on conditions of repentance: "And now, there was no means to reclaim men from this fallen state, which man had brought upon himself because of his own disobedience;

"Therefore, according to justice, the plan of redemption could not be brought about, only on conditions of repentance of men in this probationary state, yea, this preparatory state; for except it were for these conditions, mercy could not take effect except it should destroy the work of justice. Now the work of justice could not be destroyed; if so, God would cease to be God" (Alma 42:12–13).

Alma then described the roles that law, sin, punishment, remorse of conscience, repentance, justice, and mercy play in the Atonement: "And thus we see that all mankind were fallen, and they were in the grasp of justice; yea, the justice of God, which consigned them forever to be cut off from his presence.

"And now, the plan of mercy could not be brought about except an atonement should be made; therefore God himself atoneth for the sins of the world, to bring about the plan of mercy, to appease the demands of justice, that God might be a perfect, just God, and a merciful God also.

"Now, repentance could not come unto men except there were a punishment, which also was eternal as the life of the soul should be, affixed opposite to the plan of happiness, which was as eternal also as the life of the soul.

"Now, how could a man repent except he should sin? How could he sin if there was no law? How could there be a law save there was a punishment? Now, there was a punishment affixed, and a just law given, which brought remorse of conscience unto man.

"Now, if there was no law given—if a man murdered he should die—would he be afraid he would die if he should murder? And also, if there was no law given against sin men would not be afraid to sin. And if there was no law given, if men sinned what could justice do, or mercy either, for they would have no claim upon the creature?

"But there is a law given, and a punishment affixed, and a repentance granted; which repentance, mercy claimeth; otherwise, justice claimeth the creature and executeth the law, and the law inflicteth the punishment; if not so, the works of justice would be destroyed, and God would cease to be God.

"But God ceaseth not to be God, and mercy claimeth the penitent, and mercy cometh because of the atonement; and the atonement bringeth to pass the resurrection of the dead; and the resurrection of the dead bringeth back men into the presence of God; and thus they are restored into his presence, to be judged according to their works, according to the law and justice" (Alma 42:14–23).

Verses 24–25 are a sobering reminder that unless we qualify for mercy, justice will prevail: "For behold, justice exerciseth all his demands, and also mercy claimeth all which is her own; and thus, none but the truly penitent are saved. What, do ye suppose that mercy can rob justice? I say unto you, Nay; not one whit. If so, God would cease to be God."

Every seeker of truth should study, ponder, analyze, and pray about the comprehensive information contained in Alma 42. It contains truths that can be discovered only through diligent study.

President John Taylor explained some of the true doctrines of salvation revealed in this scripture: "The Savior thus becomes master of the situation—the debt is paid, the redemption made, the covenant fulfilled, justice satisfied, the will of God done, and all power is now given into the hands of the Son of God—the power of the resurrection, the power of the redemption, the power of salvation, the power to enact laws for the carrying out and accomplishment of this design. Hence life and immortality are brought to light, the Gospel is introduced, and He becomes the author of eternal life and exaltation, He is the Redeemer, the Resurrector, the Savior of man and the world; and He has appointed the law of the Gospel as the medium which must be complied with in this world or the next, as He complied with His Father's law; hence 'he that believeth shall be saved, and he that believeth not shall be damned' [D&C 68:9; D&C 112:29; Mark 16:16].

"The plan, the arrangement, the agreement, the covenant was made, entered into and accepted before the foundation of the world; it was prefigured by sacrifices, and was carried out and consummated on the cross.

"Hence being the mediator between God and man, He becomes by right the dictator and director on earth and in heaven for the living and for the dead, for the past, the present and the future, pertaining to man as associated with this earth or the heavens, in time or eternity, the Captain of our salvation, the Apostle and High-Priest of our profession, the Lord and Giver of life.

"Is justice dishonored? No; it is satisfied, the debt is paid. Is righteousness departed from? No; this is a righteous act. All requirements are met. Is judgment violated? No; its demands are fulfilled.

Is mercy triumphant? No; she simply claims her own. Justice, judgment, mercy and truth all harmonize as the attributes of Deity. . . . Justice and judgment triumph as well as mercy and peace; all the attributes of Deity harmonize in this great, grand, momentous, just, equitable, merciful and meritorious act."[4]

MERCY AND JUSTICE

We must clearly understand justice and mercy if we wish to know how the Atonement works in our life. What is justice? What is mercy? Consider this analogy:

A loving father and mother direct their thirteen-year-old son to wash the dishes, sweep the floor, and clean his room while they are gone from the home for several hours. When they return, none of the assigned tasks has been performed by the son. The parents had established certain rules, or laws, that governed their son. The son broke the laws by his noncompliance. This could be deemed sin, or transgression of the law.

The parents, who deeply love their son and desire that he be obedient, must consider some form of punishment for him. They restrict their son to his room and deny him certain privileges for several days. This is justice. The son is punished for his disobedience, and the justice of his parents on his behalf exercises control in his life.

During the period of justice, the son had planned on visiting a friend, but the justice of the parents prevents that from happening. The son begins to feel remorse for his disobedient acts. He wishes he had done the tasks assigned to him by his parents. He could then visit his friend. But he is subject to the justice of his parents, and his punishment is greater than he wishes to bear.

How can he overcome this justice? Can he simply ask his parents to cancel it? Remember Alma 42:25: "What, do ye suppose that mercy can rob justice? I say unto you, Nay; not one whit. If so, God would cease to be God."

The son must make himself eligible for the mercy of his parents. He must repent. He must become penitent. "For behold, justice exerciseth all his demands, and also mercy claimeth all which is her own; and thus, none but the truly penitent are saved" (Alma 42:24).

The son approaches his parents and seeks their forgiveness. He apologizes for his wrongdoing. He agrees to perform all of the assigned tasks, plus several other duties the parents would like him to do. Has mercy robbed justice? No! The repentance of the son has satisfied the demands of justice and made him eligible for the mercy of his parents. The parents control and mete out both justice and mercy.

"And thus mercy can satisfy the demands of justice, and encircles them in the arms of safety, while he that exercises no faith unto repentance is exposed to the whole law of the demands of justice; therefore only unto him that has faith unto repentance is brought about the great and eternal plan of redemption" (Alma 34:16).

To be unrepentant is to be ineligible for mercy. Justice will prevail: "Therefore if that man repenteth not, and remaineth and dieth an enemy to God, the demands of divine justice do awaken his immortal soul to a lively sense of his own guilt, which doth cause him to shrink from the presence of the Lord, and doth fill his breast with guilt, and pain, and anguish, which is like an unquenchable fire, whose flame ascendeth up forever and ever. And now I say unto you, that mercy hath no claim on that man; therefore his final doom is to endure a never-ending torment" (Mosiah 2:38–39).

To be repentant is to qualify for mercy: "And moreover, I would desire that ye should consider on the blessed and happy state of those that keep the commandments of God. For behold, they are blessed in all things, both temporal and spiritual; and if they hold out faithful to the end they are received into heaven, that thereby they may dwell with God in a state of never-ending happiness. O remember, remember that these things are true; for the Lord God hath spoken it" (Mosiah 2:41).

The miracle of repentance and forgiveness is beautifully illustrated in excerpts from letters written by young members of the Church who confessed to priesthood leaders as part of repenting of immoral activities.

EXAMPLE ONE

"I owe the Savior everything I have. I will be in debt to my Redeemer for all eternity because of his love and merciful arm that was extending out to me when I had lost my way. Where would I be without the Savior? How could I cleanse myself without my Redeemer? Because I am in debt to my Savior forever for what he has done for me, I have a desire to serve the Lord with all my heart, might, mind, and strength."

EXAMPLE TWO

"I know with powerful certainty that without his atoning sacrifice, I would still be lost in that vile and sinful state, being shackled to those pernicious sins for all eternity. Yet through the miracle of repentance I have been purified and cleansed of those sins and have received forgiveness from Heavenly Father."

EXAMPLE THREE

"The greatest change or addition in my life has been a great appreciation for the Atonement. Throughout my life I have thought of the Atonement as another lesson in the teaching manual. Now the Atonement is real to me. The Atonement has given me a new life, an opportunity to begin again, clean and worthy. I will never be able to fully understand the sacrifice and pain our Savior endured, but I will always be grateful for him and his pure love. I also will never be able to repay my Heavenly Father or Jesus Christ for all they have given me, but I will continue to try."

Elder Dallin H. Oaks, in remarks to General Authorities, described justice and mercy: "Justice has many meanings to men. One is balance. The symbol of justice is a scales in balance. Similarly, *justice* in an exchange signifies equivalence on each side.

"*Justice* also connotes a result that is merited or right. Thus, when we say that a person has received justice, we usually mean that he has received what he deserved.

"Another meaning for *justice* is 'fairness.' A just result is a fair result. Fairness should produce justice.

"In terms of fairness, the justice of God is manifest in the assurance that all mankind will be judged 'not according to what they have not, but according to what they have, those who have lived without law will be judged without law, and those who have a law, will be judged by that law' (*Teachings of the Prophet Joseph Smith*, 218). Thus, the Book of Mormon prophets told the Nephites that because of the teachings they had received their behavior was potentially more deserving of eternal punishment than the Lamanites. The Lamanites were ignorant and sinful 'because of the traditions of their fathers' (Alma 9:16). If the Nephites were to 'transgress contrary to the light and knowledge which they do have . . . it would be far more tolerable for the Lamanites than for them' (Alma 9:23; see also Hel. 7:23–24; 15:15–17).

"*Mercy* signifies an advantage greater than is deserved. This could come by the withholding of a deserved punishment or by the granting of an undeserved benefit. If justice is balance, then mercy is imbalance. If justice is just what one deserves, then mercy is *more* than one deserves.

"In its relationship to justice and mercy, the *atonement* is the means by which justice is served and mercy is extended."[5]

THE MEDIATOR

President Boyd K. Packer described the relationship of justice to mercy in a talk titled "The Mediator." He told of a debtor who owed money to a creditor. The debtor could not pay and sought mercy, or forgiveness of the debt, from the creditor. The creditor had everything to lose by forgiving the debt. He sought justice, or payment, of the debt. The controversy could not be resolved by the two persons alone but required the intervention of a third person— a friend of the debtor.

"There was once a man who wanted something very much. It seemed more important than anything else in his life. In order for him to have his desire, he incurred a great debt.

"He had been warned about going into that much debt, and particularly about his creditor. But it seemed so important for him to do what he wanted to do and to have what he wanted right now. He was sure he could pay for it later.

"So he signed a contract. He would pay it off sometime along the way. He didn't worry too much about it, for the due date seemed such a long time away. He had what he wanted now, and that was what seemed important.

"The creditor was always somewhere in the back of his mind, and he made token payments now and again, thinking somehow that the day of reckoning really would never come.

"But as it always does, the day came, and the contract fell due. The debt had not been fully paid. His creditor appeared and demanded payment in full.

"Only then did he realize that his creditor not only had the power to repossess all that he owned, but the power to cast him into prison as well.

"'I cannot pay you, for I have not the power to do so,' he confessed.

"'Then,' said the creditor, 'we will exercise the contract, take your possessions, and you shall go to prison. You agreed to that. It was your choice. You signed the contract, and now it must be enforced.'

"'Can you not extend the time or forgive the debt?' the debtor begged. 'Arrange some way for me to keep what I have and not go to prison. Surely you believe in mercy? Will you not show mercy?'

"The creditor replied, 'Mercy is always so one-sided. It would serve only you. If I show mercy to you, it will leave me unpaid. It is justice I demand. Do you believe in justice?'

"'I believed in justice when I signed the contract,' the debtor said. 'It was on my side then, for I thought it would protect me. I did not need mercy then, nor think I should need it ever. Justice, I thought, would serve both of us equally as well.'

"'It is justice that demands that you pay the contract or suffer the penalty,' the creditor replied. 'That is the law. You have agreed to it and that is the way it must be. Mercy cannot rob justice.'

"There they were: One meting out justice, the other pleading for mercy. Neither could prevail except at the expense of the other.

"'If you do not forgive the debt there will be no mercy,' the debtor pleaded.

"'If I do, there will be no justice,' was the reply.

"Both laws, it seemed, could not be served. They are two eternal ideals that appear to contradict one another. Is there no way for justice to be fully served, and mercy also?

"There is a way! The law of justice *can* be fully satisfied and

117

mercy *can* be fully extended—but it takes someone else. And so it happened this time.

"The debtor had a friend. He came to help. He knew the debtor well. He knew him to be shortsighted. He thought him foolish to have gotten himself into such a predicament. Nevertheless, he wanted to help because he loved him. He stepped between them, faced the creditor, and made this offer.

"'I will pay the debt if you will free the debtor from his contract so that he may keep his possessions and not go to prison.'

"As the creditor was pondering the offer, the mediator added, 'You demanded justice. Though he cannot pay you, I will do so. You will have been justly dealt with and can ask no more. It would not be just.'

"And so the creditor agreed.

"The mediator turned then to the debtor. 'If I pay your debt, will you accept me as your creditor?'

"'Oh yes, yes,' cried the debtor. 'You save me from prison and show mercy to me.'

"'Then,' said the benefactor, 'you will pay the debt to me and I will set the terms. It will not be easy, but it will be possible. I will provide a way. You need not go to prison.'

"And so it was that the creditor was paid in full. He had been justly dealt with. No contract had been broken.

"The debtor, in turn, had been extended mercy. Both laws stood fulfilled. Because there was a mediator, justice had claimed its full share, and mercy was fully satisfied."[6]

The mediator is Jesus Christ. Only he can appease the demands of justice with his mercy and love, provided we are willing to repent and be penitent, humble, and submissive. We must recognize the Eternal Father as the author of the plan that provides the healing power of mercy in our lives. Mercy comes because of the atoning sacrifice of Jesus Christ, the Son of God.

"And thus God breaketh the bands of death, having gained the victory over death; giving the Son power to make intercession for the children of men—

"Having ascended into heaven, having the bowels of mercy; being filled with compassion towards the children of men; standing betwixt them and justice; having broken the bands of death, taken upon himself their iniquity and their transgressions, having redeemed them, and satisfied the demands of justice" (Mosiah 15:8–9).

One of my favorite hymns puts to music the role of our Savior Jesus Christ:

> *I stand all amazed at the love Jesus offers me,*
> *Confused at the grace that so fully he proffers me.*
> *I tremble to know that for me he was crucified,*
> *That for me, a sinner, he suffered, he bled and died.*
>
> *I marvel that he would descend from his throne divine*
> *To rescue a soul so rebellious and proud as mine,*
> *That he should extend his great love unto such as I,*
> *Sufficient to own, to redeem, and to justify.*
>
> *I think of his hands pierced and bleeding to pay the debt!*
> *Such mercy, such love, and devotion can I forget?*
> *No, no, I will praise and adore at the mercy seat,*
> *Until at the glorified throne I kneel at his feet.*
>
> *Oh, it is wonderful that he should care for me*
> *Enough to die for me!*
> *Oh, it is wonderful, wonderful to me!*[7]

Notes

1. "First Presidency Extols Meaning of Christmas," *Ensign*, February 1995, 78.

2. Charles W. Penrose, *Rays of Living Light—No. 3* (n.p., n.d.), 1–2.

3. *The Discourses of Wilford Woodruff*, comp. G. Homer Durham (Salt Lake City: Bookcraft, 1946), 3–4.

4. John Taylor, *The Mediation and Atonement* (Salt Lake City: Deseret News, 1882), 171–72.

5. Dallin H. Oaks, "The Atonement and the Principles of Justice and Mercy," General Authority training meeting, 1 May 1985, 1.

6. Boyd K. Packer, *That All May Be Edified* (Salt Lake City: Bookcraft, 1982), 318–19.

7. "I Stand All Amazed," *Hymns of The Church of Jesus Christ of Latter-day Saints* (Salt Lake City: The Church of Jesus Christ of Latter-day Saints, 1985), no. 193.

VIII
LITTLE CHILDREN AND
THOSE WITHOUT LAW

One of the most wonderful doctrines of the Church is the doctrine of baptism for the dead. Another wonderful doctrine is that children under the age of accountability and persons with a diminished accountability need not be baptized to obtain salvation and become eligible for eternal life.

Many persons, whether investigators or members of the Church, have experienced the loss of a loved one who did not know of the true gospel before death. For those who have experienced the loss of a child, peace and comfort is difficult to obtain without a knowledge of the plan of salvation.

The universal application of the Atonement suggests that the blessings of the Atonement will be available to every person born on earth. The gospel plan, in its beauty and comprehensiveness, does indeed make those blessings available to all mankind.

The prophets have testified with clarity and exactness that those who die without the law and little children who die before the age of accountability are eligible for the full and complete blessings of the Atonement.

INNOCENT UNDER THE LAW

The Book of Mormon tells us that the Atonement is applicable to all who have lived without a knowledge of the law or are innocent under the law.

"Wherefore, he has given a law; and where there is no law given there is no punishment; and where there is no punishment there is no condemnation; and where there is no condemnation the mercies of the Holy One of Israel have claim upon them, because of the atonement; for they are delivered by the power of him.

"For the atonement satisfieth the demands of his justice upon all those who have not the law given to them, that they are delivered from that awful monster, death and hell, and the devil, and the lake of fire and brimstone, which is endless torment; and they are restored to that God who gave them breath, which is the Holy One of Israel" (2 Nephi 9:25–26).

"For behold, and also his blood atoneth for the sins of those who have fallen by the transgression of Adam, who have died not knowing the will of God concerning them, or who have ignorantly sinned" (Mosiah 3:11).

Many have lived and died, and many will yet live and die, without knowing of the saving principles of the gospel of Jesus Christ. For centuries, gospel administrators authorized to perform priesthood ordinances, including baptism, were not on the earth. The scriptures state clearly that those who have part in the First Resurrection include those who died before Christ came and were ignorant of his proclaimed salvation.

"And these are those who have part in the first resurrection; and these are they that have died before Christ came, in their

ignorance, not having salvation declared unto them. And thus the
Lord bringeth about the restoration of these; and they have a part
in the first resurrection, or have eternal life, being redeemed by the
Lord" (Mosiah 15:24).

In 1836, the Prophet Joseph Smith received a marvelous vision
wherein he was taught that those who died without a knowledge of
the gospel and who would have received it had it been available to
them will be heirs of the celestial kingdom. This revelation had particular significance to the Prophet because his brother Alvin had
passed away before the gospel was restored. Joseph saw Alvin in the
beauty of the celestial kingdom.

"The heavens were opened upon us, and I beheld the celestial
kingdom of God, and the glory thereof, whether in the body or out
I cannot tell.

"I saw the transcendent beauty of the gate through which the
heirs of that kingdom will enter, which was like unto circling flames
of fire; also the blazing throne of God, whereon was seated the
Father and the Son. I saw the beautiful streets of that kingdom,
which had the appearance of being paved with gold.

"I saw Father Adam and Abraham; and my father and my
mother; my brother Alvin, that has long since slept; and marveled
how it was that he had obtained an inheritance in that kingdom,
seeing that he had departed this life before the Lord had set his
hand to gather Israel the second time, and had not been baptized
for the remission of sins.

"Thus came the voice of the Lord unto me, saying: All who
have died without a knowledge of this gospel, who would have
received it if they had been permitted to tarry, shall be heirs of the
celestial kingdom of God; also all that shall die henceforth without
a knowledge of it, who would have received it with all their hearts,

shall be heirs of that kingdom; for I, the Lord, will judge all men according to their works, according to the desire of their hearts.

"And I also beheld that all children who die before they arrive at the years of accountability are saved in the celestial kingdom of heaven" (D&C 137:1–10).

President Joseph F. Smith received a similar revelation on the state of those who have died without knowing or accepting the gospel. He saw how the Lord organized his forces to teach the gospel to those who died without the law.

"Thus was the gospel preached to those who had died in their sins, without a knowledge of the truth, or in transgression, having rejected the prophets.

"These were taught faith in God, repentance from sin, vicarious baptism for the remission of sins, the gift of the Holy Ghost by the laying on of hands, and all other principles of the gospel that were necessary for them to know in order to qualify themselves that they might be judged according to men in the flesh, but live according to God in the spirit.

"And so it was made known among the dead, both small and great, the unrighteous as well as the faithful, that redemption had been wrought through the sacrifice of the Son of God upon the cross" (D&C 138:32–35).

The sacred principle and practice of baptism for the dead, as understood, taught, and implemented by The Church of Jesus Christ of Latter-day Saints, bears witness that God is the God of all mankind. All are invited to hear the word and be taught the saving principles of the gospel of Jesus Christ. If not, God would be a partial God, which he is not.

In the New Testament, Paul asked, "Else what shall they do which are baptized for the dead, if the dead rise not at all? why are they then baptized for the dead?" (1 Corinthians 15:29). His questions are best answered through modern revelation.

"For a baptismal font there is not upon the earth, that they, my saints, may be baptized for those who are dead—for this ordinance belongeth to my house, and cannot be acceptable to me, only in the days of your poverty, wherein ye are not able to build a house unto me.

"But I command you, all ye my saints, to build a house unto me; and I grant unto you a sufficient time to build a house unto me; and during this time your baptisms shall be acceptable unto me.

"But behold, at the end of this appointment your baptisms for your dead shall not be acceptable unto me; and if you do not these things at the end of the appointment ye shall be rejected as a church, with your dead, saith the Lord your God.

"For verily I say unto you, that after you have had sufficient time to build a house to me, wherein the ordinance of baptizing for the dead belongeth, and for which the same was instituted from before the foundation of the world, your baptisms for your dead cannot be acceptable unto me; for therein are the keys of the holy priesthood ordained, that you may receive honor and glory" (D&C 124:29–34).

LITTLE CHILDREN

The scriptures clarify how the Atonement applies to little children under the age of accountability who are not capable of sinning, to those who have not been given the law, and to those for whom the law does not apply, including adults who are not mentally accountable.

"And many signs, and wonders, and types, and shadows showed he unto them, concerning his coming; and also holy prophets spake unto them concerning his coming; and yet they hardened their hearts, and understood not that the law of Moses availeth nothing except it were through the atonement of his blood.

"And even if it were possible that little children could sin they could not be saved; but I say unto you they are blessed; for behold, as in Adam, or by nature, they fall, even so the blood of Christ atoneth for their sins.

"And moreover, I say unto you, that there shall be no other name given nor any other way nor means whereby salvation can come unto the children of men, only in and through the name of Christ, the Lord Omnipotent" (Mosiah 3:15–17).

"Listen to the words of Christ, your Redeemer, your Lord and your God. Behold, I came into the world not to call the righteous but sinners to repentance; the whole need no physician, but they that are sick; wherefore, little children are whole, for they are not capable of committing sin; wherefore the curse of Adam is taken from them in me, that it hath no power over them; and the law of circumcision is done away in me.

"And after this manner did the Holy Ghost manifest the word of God unto me; wherefore, my beloved son, I know that it is solemn mockery before God, that ye should baptize little children.

"Behold I say unto you that this thing shall ye teach—repentance and baptism unto those who are accountable and capable of committing sin; yea, teach parents that they must repent and be baptized, and humble themselves as their little children, and they shall all be saved with their little children.

"And their little children need no repentance, neither baptism. Behold, baptism is unto repentance to the fulfilling the commandments unto the remission of sins. But little children are alive in Christ, even from the foundation of the world; if not so, God is a partial God, and also a changeable God, and a respecter to persons; for how many little children have died without baptism!

"Wherefore, if little children could not be saved without baptism, these must have gone to an endless hell. Behold I say unto you, that he that supposeth that little children need baptism is in the gall of bitterness and in the bonds of iniquity; for he hath neither faith, hope, nor charity; wherefore, should he be cut off while in the thought, he must go down to hell. . . .

"Little children cannot repent; wherefore, it is awful wickedness to deny the pure mercies of God unto them, for they are all alive in him because of his mercy. And he that saith that little children need baptism denieth the mercies of Christ, and setteth at naught the atonement of him and the power of his redemption.

"Wo unto such, for they are in danger of death, hell, and an endless torment. I speak it boldly; God hath commanded me. Listen unto them and give heed, or they stand against you at the judgment-seat of Christ.

"For behold that all little children are alive in Christ, and also all they that are without the law. For the power of redemption cometh on all them that have no law; wherefore, he that is not condemned, or he that is under no condemnation, cannot repent; and unto such baptism availeth nothing—

"But it is mockery before God, denying the mercies of Christ, and the power of his Holy Spirit, and putting trust in dead works. Behold, my son, this thing ought not to be; for repentance is unto them that are under condemnation and under the curse of a broken law" (Moroni 8:8–14, 19–24).

"But behold, I say unto you, that little children are redeemed from the foundation of the world through mine Only Begotten; wherefore, they cannot sin, for power is not given unto Satan to tempt little children, until they begin to become accountable before me; for it is given unto them even as I will, according to mine own pleasure, that great things may be required at the hand of their fathers.

"And, again, I say unto you, that whoso having knowledge, have I not commanded to repent? And he that hath no understanding, it remaineth in me to do according as it is written. And now I declare no more unto you at this time. Amen" (D&C 29:46–50).

"The doctrine of baptizing children, or sprinkling them, or they must welter in hell, is a doctrine not true, not supported in Holy Writ, and is not consistent with the character of God. All children are redeemed by the blood of Jesus Christ, and the moment that children leave this world, they are taken to the bosom of Abraham. The only difference between the old and young dying is, one lives longer in heaven and eternal light and glory than the other, and is freed a little sooner from this miserable wicked world."[1]

"Wherefore, he has given a law; and where there is no law given there is no punishment; and where there is no punishment there is no condemnation; and where there is no condemnation the mercies of the Holy One of Israel have claim upon them, because of the atonement; for they are delivered by the power of him.

"For the atonement satisfieth the demands of his justice upon all those who have not the law given to them, that they are delivered from that awful monster, death and hell, and the devil, and the lake of fire and brimstone, which is endless torment; and they are restored to that God who gave them breath, which is the Holy One of Israel" (2 Nephi 9:25–26).

THE AGE OF ACCOUNTABILITY

The Lord has revealed that the age of accountability for children is eight: "And again, inasmuch as parents have children in Zion, or in any of her stakes which are organized, that teach them not to understand the doctrine of repentance, faith in Christ the Son of the living God, and of baptism and the gift of the Holy Ghost by the laying on of the hands, when eight years old, the sin be upon the heads of the parents.

"For this shall be a law unto the inhabitants of Zion, or in any of her stakes which are organized. And their children shall be baptized for the remission of their sins when eight years old, and receive the laying on of the hands" (D&C 68:25–27).

Because children begin their lives pure and innocent, they have the potential and opportunity for eternal life.

"Every spirit of man was innocent in the beginning; and God having redeemed man from the fall, men became again, in their infant state, innocent before God" (D&C 93:38).

"And these are those who have part in the first resurrection; and these are they that have died before Christ came, in their ignorance, not having salvation declared unto them. And thus the Lord bringeth about the restoration of these; and they have a part in the first resurrection, or have eternal life, being redeemed by the Lord. And little children also have eternal life" (Mosiah 15:24–25).

King Benjamin told us: "And even if it were possible that little children could sin they could not be saved; but I say unto you they are blessed; for behold, as in Adam, or by nature, they fall, even so the blood of Christ atoneth for their sins. . . .

"For behold he judgeth, and his judgment is just; and the infant perisheth not that dieth in his infancy; but men drink damnation to their own souls except they humble themselves and become as little children, and believe that salvation was, and is, and is to come, in and through the atoning blood of Christ, the Lord Omnipotent" (Mosiah 3:16, 18).

I know of a large family that lost one of their children in infancy. The child was denied a Christian funeral and burial because, according to the family minister, the infant had not been baptized prior to its untimely death. Several years later, when missionaries knocked on the door of this family's home, the father asked only one question of the missionaries. "What does your Church teach concerning the fate of children who have not been baptized and die as infants?"

The missionaries testified of the Atonement, the redemption of little children by the grace of Jesus Christ, and of the fact that little children need not be baptized but are saved because they are without sin. The family immediately joined the Church and became at peace with the true doctrine regarding innocent children and the Atonement.

"Adam fell that men might be; and men are, that they might have joy. And the Messiah cometh in the fulness of time, that he may redeem the children of men from the fall. And because that they are redeemed from the fall they have become free forever, knowing good from evil; to act for themselves and not to be acted upon, save it be by the punishment of the law at the great and last day, according to the commandments which God hath given" (2 Nephi 2:25–26).

NOTE

1. *Teachings of the Prophet Joseph Smith*, sel. Joseph Fielding Smith (Salt Lake City: Deseret Book, 1976), 197.

IX
COMMANDMENTS, COVENANTS, AND ORDINANCES

Those who have accepted the gospel and been baptized members of the Church have a responsibility to make and keep sacred covenants. They enter into covenants by participation in ordinances administered under the direction of priesthood leaders who hold the keys of administering the ordinances.

Contrary to the practice of some religious groups, The Church of Jesus Christ of Latter-day Saints teaches that salvation and exaltation require more than a one-time statement of belief in Jesus Christ or a declaration of being "saved" without further obligation. An understanding of the plan of redemption brings with it a responsibility to keep the commandments. This responsibility is for life.

To "endure to the end" is a principle of the gospel. Understanding and keeping the commandments requires that we make a resolution to overcome Satan's influences and temptations. Commandments become covenants with God when we acknowledge to God, through ordinances, that we will keep the commandments. Much has been revealed in holy scripture about this subject.

KING BENJAMIN'S MESSAGE

King Benjamin's address in the first four chapters of the book of Mosiah is one of the greatest sermons ever given and recorded. Elder Jeffrey R. Holland described it as "a magnificent discourse on Christ's suffering and atonement, the role of justice and mercy, and the need to take upon ourselves the name of Christ in a covenantal relationship."[1]

This sermon is often referred to for its reference to service: "And behold, I tell you these things that ye may learn wisdom; that ye may learn that when ye are in the service of your fellow beings ye are only in the service of your God" (Mosiah 2:17). King Benjamin's message, however, extends far beyond that principle. He taught us to qualify for the Atonement by keeping the commandments of God.

"And moreover, I would desire that ye should consider on the blessed and happy state of those that keep the commandments of God. For behold, they are blessed in all things, both temporal and spiritual; and if they hold out faithful to the end they are received into heaven, that thereby they may dwell with God in a state of never-ending happiness. O remember, remember that these things are true; for the Lord God hath spoken it" (Mosiah 2:41).

The Atonement and its attendant mercy have no claim on a sinful person who fails to repent: "And now, I say unto you, my brethren, that after ye have known and have been taught all these things, if ye should transgress and go contrary to that which has been spoken, that ye do withdraw yourselves from the Spirit of the Lord, that it may have no place in you to guide you in wisdom's paths that ye may be blessed, prospered, and preserved—

"I say unto you, that the man that doeth this, the same cometh out in open rebellion against God; therefore he listeth to obey the evil spirit, and becometh an enemy to all righteousness; therefore, the Lord has no place in him, for he dwelleth not in unholy temples.

"Therefore if that man repenteth not, and remaineth and dieth an enemy to God, the demands of divine justice do awaken his immortal soul to a lively sense of his own guilt, which doth cause him to shrink from the presence of the Lord, and doth fill his breast with guilt, and pain, and anguish, which is like an unquenchable fire, whose flame ascendeth up forever and ever.

"And now I say unto you, that mercy hath no claim on that man; therefore his final doom is to endure a never-ending torment" (Mosiah 2:36–39).

King Benjamin foretold the coming of Jesus Christ in the flesh and the singular means by which mankind can be saved: "And moreover, I say unto you, that there shall be no other name given nor any other way nor means whereby salvation can come unto the children of men, only in and through the name of Christ, the Lord Omnipotent.

"For behold he judgeth, and his judgment is just; and the infant perisheth not that dieth in his infancy; but men drink damnation to their own souls except they humble themselves and become as little children, and believe that salvation was, and is, and is to come, in and through the atoning blood of Christ, the Lord Omnipotent.

"For the natural man is an enemy to God, and has been from the fall of Adam, and will be, forever and ever, unless he yields to the enticings of the Holy Spirit, and putteth off the natural man and becometh a saint through the atonement of Christ the Lord, and becometh as a child, submissive, meek, humble, patient, full of love, willing to submit to all things which the Lord seeth fit to inflict upon him, even as a child doth submit to his father.

"And moreover, I say unto you, that the time shall come when the knowledge of a Savior shall spread throughout every nation, kindred, tongue, and people" (Mosiah 3:17–20).

King Benjamin's people were warned so powerfully that they fell to the earth, "for the fear of the Lord had come upon them. And they had viewed themselves in their own carnal state, even less than the dust of the earth. And they all cried aloud with one voice, saying: O have mercy, and apply the atoning blood of Christ that we may receive forgiveness of our sins, and our hearts may be purified; for we believe in Jesus Christ, the Son of God, who created heaven and earth, and all things; who shall come down among the children of men.

"And it came to pass that after they had spoken these words the Spirit of the Lord came upon them, and they were filled with joy, having received a remission of their sins, and having peace of conscience, because of the exceeding faith which they had in Jesus Christ who should come, according to the words which king Benjamin had spoken unto them."

King Benjamin then declared unto his people: "I say unto you, if ye have come to a knowledge of the goodness of God, and his matchless power, and his wisdom, and his patience, and his long-suffering towards the children of men; and also, the atonement which has been prepared from the foundation of the world, that thereby salvation might come to him that should put his trust in the Lord, and should be diligent in keeping his commandments, and continue in the faith even unto the end of his life, I mean the life of the mortal body—

"I say, that this is the man who receiveth salvation, through the atonement which was prepared from the foundation of the world for all mankind, which ever were since the fall of Adam, or who are, or who ever shall be, even unto the end of the world.

"And this is the means whereby salvation cometh. And there is none other salvation save this which hath been spoken of; neither are there any conditions whereby man can be saved except the conditions which I have told you.

"Believe in God; believe that he is, and that he created all things, both in heaven and in earth; believe that he has all wisdom, and all power, both in heaven and in earth; believe that man doth not comprehend all the things which the Lord can comprehend.

"And again, believe that ye must repent of your sins and forsake them, and humble yourselves before God; and ask in sincerity of heart that he would forgive you; and now, if you believe all these things see that ye do them.

"And again I say unto you as I have said before, that as ye have come to the knowledge of the glory of God, or if ye have known of his goodness and have tasted of his love, and have received a remission of your sins, which causeth such exceedingly great joy in your souls, even so I would that ye should remember, and always retain in remembrance, the greatness of God, and your own nothingness, and his goodness and long-suffering towards you, unworthy creatures, and humble yourselves even in the depths of humility, calling on the name of the Lord daily, and standing steadfastly in the faith of that which is to come, which was spoken by the mouth of the angel.

"And behold, I say unto you that if ye do this ye shall always rejoice, and be filled with the love of God, and always retain a remission of your sins; and ye shall grow in the knowledge of the glory of him that created you, or in the knowledge of that which is just and true. . . .

"And finally, I cannot tell you all the things whereby ye may commit sin; for there are divers ways and means, even so many that I cannot number them. But this much I can tell you, that if ye do not watch yourselves, and your thoughts, and your words, and your deeds, and observe the commandments of God, and continue in the faith of what ye have heard concerning the coming of our Lord, even unto the end of your lives, ye must perish. And now, O man, remember, and perish not" (Mosiah 4:1–3, 6–12, 29–30).

King Benjamin taught that salvation comes because of the Atonement. When we exercise faith in God, repent, are baptized, and participate in essential ordinances, we receive a remission of our sins. The necessity of keeping and observing the commandments of God is central to the message of this venerable prophet.

KEEPING THE COMMANDMENTS

All prophets have taught us to keep the commandments. There is safety in keeping the commandments. Keeping the commandments may be difficult, but the scriptures teach us that the commandments were *not* given until *after* the plan of redemption was made known.

"Therefore God gave unto them commandments, after having made known unto them the plan of redemption" (Alma 12:32).

The key word in the above verse is *after*. The commandments were not given until *after* the plan of redemption was made known. When a missionary is teaching an investigator about the restored gospel, the investigator must have the beginning of an understanding of the plan of salvation before being taught the commandments. When children are taught rules and commandments to observe in the home, they often ask why. The answer is found in the Book of Mormon:

"Therefore, whosoever repenteth, and hardeneth not his heart, he shall have claim on mercy through mine Only Begotten Son, unto a remission of his sins; and these shall enter into my rest. And whosoever will harden his heart and will do iniquity, behold, I swear in my wrath that he shall not enter into my rest" (Alma 12:34–35).

So that men would not be subject to spiritual death, or death as to righteousness, God prepared a plan whereby he would have mercy on those who repent and do not harden their hearts. Mercy satisfies the demands of justice for those who repent. We repent by forsaking sin and keeping commandments. The Lord patiently teaches why we must keep his commandments and how his plan of redemption is the basis for keeping the commandments.

Following his marvelous sermon, King Benjamin desired to know if the people believed his words: "And they all cried with one voice, saying: Yea, we believe all the words which thou hast spoken unto us; and also, we know of their surety and truth, because of the Spirit of the Lord Omnipotent, which has wrought a mighty change in us, or in our hearts, that we have no more disposition to do evil, but to do good continually" (Mosiah 5:2).

The lives of the people had been so deeply affected by the king's words that a mighty change was wrought in their hearts. They no longer were disposed to do evil but wanted only to do good continually.

ESSENTIAL ORDINANCES AND COVENANTS

All ordinances are sacred acts. Certain ordinances are referred to as saving ordinances. They include baptism and confirmation. For men, ordination to the Melchizedek Priesthood is essential for exaltation; for all accountable persons, the temple endowment and a temple sealing are required for exaltation. Whenever we participate in an ordinance, we make a covenant with God.

The commitment of King Benjamin's people to do good and to

keep the commandments he had given them led to their desire to enter into covenants with God: "And we are willing to enter into a covenant with our God to do his will, and to be obedient to his commandments in all things that he shall command us, all the remainder of our days, that we may not bring upon ourselves a never-ending torment, as has been spoken by the angel, that we may not drink out of the cup of the wrath of God" (Mosiah 5:5).

The people covenanted to "be called the children of Christ," being "born of him" and becoming "his sons and his daughters" (Mosiah 5:7). They also covenanted to take "upon [themselves] the name of Christ, . . . that [they] should be obedient [to God] unto the end of their lives" (Mosiah 5:8).

King Benjamin told the people that he who entered into the sacred covenants "shall know the name by which he is called; for he shall be called by the name of Christ" (Mosiah 5:9). And "whosoever shall not take upon him the name of Christ must be called by some other name; therefore, he findeth himself on the left hand of God" (Mosiah 5:10).

Elder Bruce R. McConkie offered a definition of a covenant: "In the gospel sense, a *covenant* is a binding and solemn compact, agreement, contract, or mutual promise between God and a single person or a group of chosen persons. (D&C 5:3, 27–28; 54:4.) Since God is a party to every gospel covenant, it follows that his mind and will must be known with respect to the particular contractual relationship involved. Hence, covenants come only by revelation, and no person or group of persons enters into a gospel covenant except on the basis of direct revelation from God.

"It follows that, as far as men now living are concerned, the only ones who have entered into covenants with the Lord are the members of The Church of Jesus Christ of Latter-day Saints. Their prophets are the only spiritual leaders receiving revelation for the

Church and the world, and the saints themselves are the only ones enjoying the companionship of the Holy Ghost so that personal revelation may be received. Ancient and modern scriptures contain a record of many of the covenants of the past and the present."[2]

We enter into and commit to keep many covenants, a process that Nephi delighted in: "And also my soul delighteth in the covenants of the Lord which he hath made to our fathers; yea, my soul delighteth in his grace, and in his justice, and power, and mercy in the great and eternal plan of deliverance from death" (2 Nephi 11:5).

BAPTISM—THE FIRST ORDINANCE

Our first ordinance of salvation, administered by a legal representative of the Lord, is baptism. Elder McConkie stated that by being baptized, "an individual signs his name to the *contract of salvation*."[3]

Repentance and baptism are required of all men before the full blessings of the Atonement can take effect in their lives: "And he commandeth all men that they must repent, and be baptized in his name, having perfect faith in the Holy One of Israel, or they cannot be saved in the kingdom of God. And if they will not repent and believe in his name, and be baptized in his name, and endure to the end, they must be damned; for the Lord God, the Holy One of Israel, has spoken it" (2 Nephi 9:23–24).

A commitment to repent of all sins and to serve God is a precondition of baptism. Modern-day revelation gives the qualifications for baptism:

"And again, by way of commandment to the church concerning the manner of baptism—All those who humble themselves before God, and desire to be baptized, and come forth with broken hearts and contrite spirits, and witness before the church that they have truly repented of all their sins, and are willing to take upon them the name of Jesus Christ, having a determination to serve him to the end, and truly manifest by their works that they have received of the Spirit of Christ unto the remission of their sins, shall be received by baptism into his church" (D&C 20:37).

Similar qualifications were required anciently: "Neither did they receive any unto baptism save they came forth with a broken heart and a contrite spirit, and witnessed unto the church that they truly repented of all their sins. And none were received unto baptism save they took upon them the name of Christ, having a determination to serve him to the end.

"And after they had been received unto baptism, and were wrought upon and cleansed by the power of the Holy Ghost, they were numbered among the people of the church of Christ; and their names were taken, that they might be remembered and nourished by the good word of God, to keep them in the right way, to keep them continually watchful unto prayer, relying alone upon the merits of Christ, who was the author and the finisher of their faith" (Moroni 6:2–4).

The doctrine of baptism—its symbolism and absolute necessity as the first ordinance of salvation relating to the Atonement—is one of the clearest doctrines taught in the scriptures.

"Baptism is the rite and procedure, given of God, whereby men may be reconciled to him through the atonement of his Only Begotten Son. The gospel itself is the new and everlasting covenant, the covenant Deity makes with men to save them with an eternal salvation. Those who believe and obey gain salvation through the atonement. Baptism as a new and an everlasting covenant is the means whereby each individual signifies his acceptance of the gospel covenant. In baptism each person signs, as it were, the contractual agreement; he promises to live by gospel standards, and the Lord promises to pour out upon him all of the blessings of the gospel, the chief of which is eternal life. Baptism and the resultant conformity to the Lord's laws thus comprise 'the doctrine of Christ, and the only and true doctrine of the Father, and of the Son, and of the Holy Ghost.' (2 Nephi 31:21.)"[4]

The ordinance of baptism is performed by a worthy priesthood holder (a priest in the Aaronic Priesthood or a holder of the Melchizedek Priesthood) who has received authorization to baptize from one who holds keys. Proper baptism also requires that the repentant, humble recipient be submerged in water. The ordinance of laying on of hands for the gift of the Holy Ghost and the confirmation of a new member into the Church follows the ordinance of baptism and is performed only by those who hold the Melchizedek Priesthood.

In the Pearl of Great Price, we read of father Adam inquiring of the Lord with respect to baptism: "And our father Adam spake unto the Lord, and said: Why is it that men must repent and be baptized in water? And the Lord said unto Adam: Behold I have forgiven thee thy transgression in the Garden of Eden.

"Hence came the saying abroad among the people, that the Son of God hath atoned for original guilt, wherein the sins of the parents cannot be answered upon the heads of the children, for they are whole from the foundation of the world.

"And the Lord spake unto Adam, saying: Inasmuch as thy children are conceived in sin, even so when they begin to grow up, sin conceiveth in their hearts, and they taste the bitter, that they may know to prize the good. And it is given unto them to know good from evil; wherefore they are agents unto themselves, and I have given unto you another law and commandment.

"Wherefore teach it unto your children, that all men, everywhere, must repent, or they can in nowise inherit the kingdom of

God, for no unclean thing can dwell there, or dwell in his presence; for, in the language of Adam, Man of Holiness is his name, and the name of his Only Begotten is the Son of Man, even Jesus Christ, a righteous Judge, who shall come in the meridian of time" (Moses 6:53–57).

No responsibility for original sin rests upon mankind. The Son of God has atoned for the transgression, or original sin, of Adam and Eve. But proper use of agency remains the responsibility of each person. When we become accountable and sin, a remission of our sins is available only through repentance and baptism. Without repentance, there is no inheritance in the kingdom of God.

UNDERSTANDING BAPTISM

The book of Moses describes baptism in symbolic terms that coincide in a marvelous way with the actual ordinance of baptism and with the process of birth: "Therefore I give unto you a commandment, to teach these things freely unto your children, saying: That by reason of transgression cometh the fall, which fall bringeth death, and inasmuch as ye were born into the world by water, and blood, and the spirit, which I have made, and so became of dust a living soul, even so ye must be born again into the kingdom of heaven, of water, and of the Spirit, and be cleansed by blood, even the blood of mine Only Begotten; that ye might be sanctified from all sin, and enjoy the words of eternal life in this world, and eternal life in the world to come, even immortal glory; for by the water ye keep the commandment; by the Spirit ye are justified, and by the blood ye are sanctified" (Moses 6:58–60).

This beautiful passage speaks of three elements associated with baptism: water, spirit, and blood. We read a similar description in the New Testament: "Who is he that overcometh the world, but he that believeth that Jesus is the Son of God? This is he that came by water and blood, even Jesus Christ; not by water only, but by water and blood. And it is the Spirit that beareth witness, because the Spirit is truth.

"For there are three that bear record in heaven, the Father, the Word, and the Holy Ghost: and these three are one. And there are three that bear witness in earth, the Spirit, and the water, and the blood: and these three agree in one" (1 John 5:5–8).

Jesus taught the need for these three essential elements of baptism to Nicodemus, a Jewish ruler: "The same came to Jesus by night, and said unto him, Rabbi, we know that thou art a teacher come from God: for no man can do these miracles that thou doest, except God be with him. Jesus answered and said unto him, Verily, verily, I say unto thee, Except a man be born again, he cannot see the kingdom of God. Nicodemus saith unto him, How can a man be born when he is old? can he enter the second time into his mother's womb, and be born? Jesus answered, Verily, verily, I say unto thee, Except a man be born of water and of the Spirit, he cannot enter into the kingdom of God" (John 3:2–5).

Nicodemus perceived baptism, or being born again, as a literal second birth, which would be impossible. Christ, of course, was describing baptism and the rebirth associated with a remission of sins, which required the elements of water, spirit, and blood.

Baptism by immersion is symbolic of a developing baby immersed in water while in its mother's womb. The baby lives and is nurtured through nutrients in its mother's blood; the nutrients reach the baby via the umbilical cord. The baby's God-given spirit provides it with life after birth.

Baptism is just as simple and beautiful. It requires immersion in water followed by a new way of life. Baptism is in the similitude of the Atonement in that the process of going down into the water and then coming forth out of the water symbolizes the death, burial, and resurrection of our Lord Jesus Christ. The efficacy of baptism is subject to the Atonement. We cannot repent and be forgiven of sins without the sacrificial blood of the Savior.

The ordinance of conferring the Holy Ghost following baptism provides the guidance of the Holy Spirit as a companion and comforter to help the newly baptized remain faithful to the end. Elder McConkie described baptism as a "once-in-a-lifetime ordinance."

"We are baptized on one occasion only—for the remission of our sins, for entrance into the earthly church, and for future admission into the kingdom of heaven. After baptism, all men sin. None obey the Lord's law in perfection; none remain clean and spotless and fit for the association of Gods and angels. But in the goodness of God, provision is made to renew and give continuing efficacy to our baptismal covenant. From Adam to the death of the Lord Jesus, baptized persons were privileged to renew all of the terms and conditions of their personal covenant of baptism through the performance of sacrificial offerings. And from the night before the crucifixion until the Lord comes again, and thereafter as long at least as the earth shall stand, baptized persons are privileged to renew their own personal covenant of salvation by partaking worthily of the sacramental emblems."[5]

In addition to the baptismal covenant that all enter into at baptism, men enter into additional covenants when they are ordained to the priesthood, and men and women enter into "the new and everlasting covenant" of marriage. Elder McConkie described the "new and everlasting covenant":

"The *new and everlasting covenant* is the fulness of the gospel and embraces within its terms and conditions every other covenant that Deity ever has made or ever will make with men. (D&C 132:5–7; 133:57.) The provisions of this covenant are that if men will believe, repent, be baptized, receive the Holy Ghost, and endure in righteousness to the end, they shall have an inheritance in the celestial world."[6]

Members of the Church may qualify to participate in certain ordinances of the gospel that are performed in holy temples. These ordinances provide worthy members an opportunity to take upon themselves specific covenants and obligations. These ordinances lead to exaltation and promised blessings for those who qualify through repentance. In addition, Church members may perform ordinances for those who have lived and died without the law.

The keys for the holy and sacred work of sealing or binding God's children in family relationships were revealed and committed to the Prophet Joseph Smith by the Old Testament prophet Elijah in the Kirtland Temple on April 3, 1836.

"After this vision had closed, another great and glorious vision burst upon us; for Elijah the prophet, who was taken to heaven without tasting death, stood before us, and said:

"Behold, the time has fully come, which was spoken of by the mouth of Malachi—testifying that he [Elijah] should be sent, before the great and dreadful day of the Lord come—to turn the hearts of the fathers to the children, and the children to the fathers, lest the whole earth be smitten with a curse—

"Therefore, the keys of this dispensation are committed into your hands; and by this ye may know that the great and dreadful day of the Lord is near, even at the doors" (D&C 110:13–16).

Other commandments and covenants deal with chastity, tithing, the Sabbath day, the Word of Wisdom, and consecration. We must understand the relationship of the sacrament of the Lord's supper to these covenants and ordinances. The wording of the sacrament prayers is found in both the Doctrine and Covenants and the Book of Mormon:

"O God, the Eternal Father, we ask thee in the name of thy

Son, Jesus Christ, to bless and sanctify this bread to the souls of all those who partake of it, that they may eat in remembrance of the body of thy Son, and witness unto thee, O God, the Eternal Father, that they are willing to take upon them the name of thy Son, and always remember him and keep his commandments which he has given them; that they may always have his Spirit to be with them. Amen" (D&C 20:77; Moroni 4:3).

"O God, the Eternal Father, we ask thee in the name of thy Son, Jesus Christ, to bless and sanctify this wine to the souls of all those who drink of it, that they may do it in remembrance of the blood of thy Son, which was shed for them; that they may witness unto thee, O God, the Eternal Father, that they do always remember him, that they may have his Spirit to be with them. Amen" (D&C 20:79; Moroni 5:2).

The covenants of these prayers closely parallel our baptismal covenants. We take upon ourselves the name of Christ, and we commit to "always remember him and keep his commandments." If we are faithful, we "may always have his Spirit to be with [us]."

When we partake of the sacrament, we renew the covenants of baptism. The sacrament is administered and passed to the members of the Church each Sunday in sacrament meeting and in fast and testimony meeting. The sacrament provides us with the frequent opportunity to remember the covenants we have made with the Lord, ponder the plan of redemption provided by our loving Heavenly Father, review the commandments we are striving to keep, and reflect on the power of the Atonement.

Modern revelation emphasizes the importance of the privilege of partaking of the sacrament: "And that thou mayest more fully keep thyself unspotted from the world, thou shalt go to the house of prayer and offer up thy sacraments upon my holy day; for verily this is a day appointed unto you to rest from your labors, and to pay thy devotions unto the Most High;

"Nevertheless thy vows shall be offered up in righteousness on all days and at all times; but remember that on this, the Lord's day, thou shalt offer thine oblations and thy sacraments unto the Most High, confessing thy sins unto thy brethren, and before the Lord.

"And on this day thou shalt do none other thing, only let thy food be prepared with singleness of heart that thy fasting may be perfect, or, in other words, that thy joy may be full" (D&C 59:9–13).

Our continued repentance, which allows mercy to satisfy the demands of the law of justice, requires that we be humble and worthy to partake of the sacrament.

Notes

1. Jeffrey R. Holland, *Christ and the New Covenant* (Salt Lake City: Deseret Book, 1997), 99.

2. Bruce R. McConkie, *Mormon Doctrine*, 2d ed. (Salt Lake City: Bookcraft, 1966), 166.

3. Bruce R. McConkie, *Mormon Doctrine*, 167.

4. Bruce R. McConkie, *A New Witness for the Articles of Faith* (Salt Lake City: Deseret Book, 1985), 242.

5. Bruce R. McConkie, *New Witness*, 293–94.

6. Bruce R. McConkie, *Mormon Doctrine*, 166–67.

X
THE LORD'S WATCHMEN TEACH US OF THE ATONEMENT

Our confidence in understanding the doctrine of the Atonement and in how the Atonement fulfills the plan of redemption established by God through his Son, Jesus Christ, comes from living prophets. To live on earth at a time when there is a living prophet who is accepted of God and through whom God can reveal his mind and will to mankind is a wonderful and marvelous blessing. Not all people in all ages have been so privileged.

Prophets live today and receive revelation from God, and the people who follow them are blessed. Satan is doing all in his power to destroy faith in Jesus Christ. Satan opposes Jesus Christ and is working to prevent us from returning to live forever with the Father and the Son. Satan carries out his plan by promoting disobedience to God's commandments, breaking of covenants, failure to participate in ordinances, and confusion about the true gospel.

God's truth will prevail over Satan's lies, thanks to ancient prophets who have left their words in recorded scripture, and thanks to latter-day prophets who teach what is right and true.

PROPHETS AND APOSTLES ARE NECESSARY

"Since the creation of man and the first revelation of God's will unto him, we have no account of the Lord ever having a people upon the earth or a system which He recognized as being His without also having men of this description—men with whom He could communicate and through whom His mind and will could be made known to the people. They were the living oracles possessing living Priesthood through which they could obtain light and intelligence from the Almighty to expound with authority to the children of men; and their words, whether delivered orally or written, were equally binding upon the people with the words of any preceding servant of God. That this was the case all sacred history bears abundant evidence.

"There cannot be a Church of Christ on the earth without having Prophets and Apostles as its officers."[1]

The prophets of God have always borne witness of the Atonement, as does the living prophet today. President Gordon B. Hinckley testified, "The greatest salient truth of life is that the Son of God came into the world and atoned for the sins of mankind and opened the gate by which we may go on to eternal life."[2]

THE INFLUENCE OF THE ADVERSARY

Even before this earth was created, the adversary—also known as the devil, Satan, or Lucifer—was promoting evil and teaching doctrines that, if believed, destroyed faith and a true understanding of the Atonement.

Beginning in the pre-earth life, Satan sought to thwart the Father's plan of the Atonement by proposing that all mankind be saved, meaning that there would be no accountability for sin or transgression. There would have been no sin under Satan's plan because agency would have been eliminated. Satan's plan was the exact opposite of the Father's plan. Christ accepted the Father's plan and became the Savior of the world, the one by whom all mankind must pass to return to the presence of the Father (2 Nephi 9:41).

In the book of Moses we read of how Satan became the devil: "And I, the Lord God, spake unto Moses, saying: That Satan, whom thou hast commanded in the name of mine Only Begotten, is the same which was from the beginning, and he came before me, saying—Behold, here am I, send me, I will be thy son, and I will redeem all mankind, that one soul shall not be lost, and surely I will do it; wherefore give me thine honor.

"But, behold, my Beloved Son, which was my Beloved and Chosen from the beginning, said unto me—Father, thy will be done, and the glory be thine forever" (Moses 4:1–2).

Satan was thinking only of himself, not of the Father's plan, when he said, "Here am *I*, send *me*, *I* will be thy son, and *I* will redeem all mankind, . . . and surely *I* will do it" (Moses 4:1; emphasis added). Satan's continual reference to himself signifies a misguided obsession with his own importance in relation to the Father. He sought to replace the Father's plan with his own plan, which would have destroyed righteousness, and he sought all the glory.

Christ, on the other hand, humbly and submissively consented to the Father's plan and sought no personal glory. He wished only to honor his Father and give him the glory forever.

Adam and Eve became the first targets of Satan's efforts to thwart the plan the Father had chosen to implement through his Beloved Son. Adam and Eve were living in the Garden of Eden and were subject to God's commandment not to partake of the forbidden fruit on penalty of death. Satan, working through the serpent, successfully enticed Eve to eat of the forbidden fruit. Adam next partook of the forbidden fruit.

"And he said unto the woman: Yea, hath God said—Ye shall not eat of every tree of the garden? (And he spake by the mouth of the serpent.)

"And the woman said unto the serpent: We may eat of the fruit of the trees of the garden; but of the fruit of the tree which thou beholdest in the midst of the garden, God hath said—Ye shall not eat of it, neither shall ye touch it, lest ye die.

"And the serpent said unto the woman: Ye shall not surely die; for God doth know that in the day ye eat thereof, then your eyes shall be opened, and ye shall be as gods, knowing good and evil.

"And when the woman saw that the tree was good for food, and that it became pleasant to the eyes, and a tree to be desired to make her wise, she took of the fruit thereof, and did eat, and also gave unto her husband with her, and he did eat" (Moses 4:7–12).

Since then, Satan has sought to destroy mankind. He is a liar and a cheat who seeks to deceive people. He offers rewards but delivers only grief and misery. As scripture tells us, "And also Satan hath sought to deceive you, that he might overthrow you" (D&C 50:3). "And he became Satan, yea, even the devil, the father of all lies, to deceive and to blind men, and to lead them captive at his will, even as many as would not hearken unto my voice" (Moses 4:4).

KORIHOR, THE ANTI-CHRIST

The followers of Satan are often referred to as "anti-Christ." The Book of Mormon chronicles the efforts of several such men who attempted to frustrate God's great plan of happiness. Chief among those characters was Korihor.

"But it came to pass in the latter end of the seventeenth year, there came a man into the land of Zarahemla, and he was Anti-Christ, for he began to preach unto the people against the prophecies which had been spoken by the prophets, concerning the coming of Christ" (Alma 30:6).

Korihor directly confronted the prophet Alma and forcefully challenged Alma's teachings to the people of Ammon: "And this Anti-Christ, whose name was Korihor, (and the law could have no hold upon him) began to preach unto the people that there should be no Christ. And after this manner did he preach, saying:

"O ye that are bound down under a foolish and a vain hope, why do ye yoke yourselves with such foolish things? Why do ye look for a Christ? For no man can know of anything which is to come.

"Behold, these things which ye call prophecies, which ye say are handed down by holy prophets, behold, they are foolish traditions of your fathers.

"How do ye know of their surety? Behold, ye cannot know of things which ye do not see; therefore ye cannot know that there shall be a Christ. Ye look forward and say that ye see a remission of your sins. But behold, it is the effect of a frenzied mind; and this derangement of your minds comes because of the traditions of your fathers, which lead you away into a belief of things which are not so.

"And many more such things did he say unto them, telling them that there could be no atonement made for the sins of men, but every man fared in this life according to the management of the creature; therefore every man prospered according to his genius, and that every man conquered according to his strength; and whatsoever a man did was no crime.

"And thus he did preach unto them, leading away the hearts of many, causing them to lift up their heads in their wickedness, yea, leading away many women, and also men, to commit whoredoms—telling them that when a man was dead, that was the end thereof" (Alma 30:12–18).

Observe the elements of Korihor's doctrine: No man can know what is to come. The prophets teach foolish traditions. Looking forward to a remission of sins is the effect of a frenzied mind. No atonement can be made for sin.

Alma boldly and with great conviction rebutted Korihor's statements: "And then Alma said unto him: Believest thou that there is a God? And he answered, Nay. Now Alma said unto him: Will ye deny again that there is a God, and also deny the Christ? For behold, I say unto you, I know there is a God, and also that Christ shall come.

"And now what evidence have ye that there is no God, or that Christ cometh not? I say unto you that ye have none, save it be your word only. But, behold, I have all things as a testimony that these things are true; and ye also have all things as a testimony unto you that they are true; and will ye deny them? Believest thou that these things are true?

"Behold, I know that thou believest, but thou art possessed with a lying spirit, and ye have put off the Spirit of God that it may have no place in you; but the devil has power over you, and he doth carry you about, working devices that he may destroy the children of God" (Alma 30:37–42).

Korihor sought for a sign as to the truthfulness of Alma's testimony and was struck dumb, remaining so throughout the remainder of his life. The lesson of Korihor is reflected in the last verse of Alma 30: "And thus we see the end of him who perverteth the ways of the Lord; and thus we see that the devil will not support his children at the last day, but doth speedily drag them down to hell" (v. 60).

PROPHETS REFUTE FALSE DOCTRINES

Lehi warned of those who teach contrary to God's true doctrines: "And if ye shall say there is no law, ye shall also say there is no sin. If ye shall say there is no sin, ye shall also say there is no righteousness. And if there be no righteousness there be no happiness. And if there be no righteousness nor happiness there be no punishment nor misery. And if these things are not there is no God. And if there is no God we are not, neither the earth; for there could have been no creation of things, neither to act nor to be acted upon; wherefore, all things must have vanished away.

"And now, my sons, I speak unto you these things for your profit and learning; for there is a God, and he hath created all things, both the heavens and the earth, and all things that in them are, both things to act and things to be acted upon" (2 Nephi 2:13–14).

Lehi showed us the logic of the anti-Christ teaching of yesterday and today. If there is no law, there is no sin. If there is no sin, there is no righteousness. If there is no righteousness, there is no happiness, punishment, or misery. If these things are true, there is no God or purpose to this earth life.

We must ever be alert to the same patterns of deception today. They are usually found among those who claim to be learned, sophisticated, or intellectually inclined. The Book of Mormon warns of such persons: "O that cunning plan of the evil one! O the vainness, and the frailties, and the foolishness of men! When they are learned they think they are wise, and they hearken not unto the counsel of God, for they set it aside, supposing they know of themselves, wherefore, their wisdom is foolishness and it profiteth them not. And they shall perish" (2 Nephi 9:28).

A WARNING TODAY

Some religious leaders maintain that The Church of Jesus Christ of Latter-day Saints is not a Christian church because our Church teaches that men and women have responsibility (beyond accepting Jesus as their Savior) for the individual salvation of their souls. These religious leaders teach that salvation means being saved by the grace of Christ only and that any work on the part of the individual is unnecessary.

How grateful we should be that modern-day prophets confirm the true doctrines of the Atonement as taught in the scriptures. The key book of scripture that explains the Atonement is the Book of Mormon. In an April 1988 general conference address, Elder Boyd K. Packer noted that despite the numerous references to the Atonement in the Old Testament in connection with the law of Moses, the word *atonement* only appears once in the New Testament. Elder Packer then observed that "in the Book of Mormon the word *atone* in form and tense appears fifty-five times . . . in the Doctrine and Covenants eleven times and in the Pearl of Great Price three times."

Elder Packer explained why the Atonement is more fully taught in the Book of Mormon and modern scripture than in the Bible: "Nephi testified that the Bible once 'contained the fulness of the gospel of the Lord, of whom the twelve apostles bear record' (1 Nephi 13:24) and that 'After [the words] go forth by the hand of the twelve apostles of the Lamb, from the Jews unto the Gentiles, thou seest the formation of that great and abominable church, which is most abominable above all other churches; for behold, they have taken away from the gospel of the Lamb many parts which are plain and most precious; and also many covenants of the Lord have they taken away' (1 Nephi 13:26).

"Jacob defined the great and abominable church in these words: 'Wherefore, he that fighteth against Zion, both Jew and Gentile, both bond and free, both male and female, shall perish; for they are they who are the whore of all the earth; for they who are not for me are against me, saith our God' (2 Nephi 10:16).

"Nephi said, 'Because of the many plain and precious things

which have been taken out of the book, . . . an exceedingly great many do stumble, yea, insomuch that Satan hath great power over them' (1 Nephi 13:29).

"He then prophesied that the precious things would be restored (see 1 Nephi 13:34–35).

"And they were restored."[3]

WATCHMEN ON THE TOWER

Today prophets stand as watchmen on the tower to warn us of danger and to teach us true doctrine. One of the most remarkable parables in scripture is found in the Doctrine and Covenants. It is the parable of the watchman on the tower.

"And now, I will show unto you a parable, that you may know my will concerning the redemption of Zion. A certain nobleman had a spot of land, very choice; and he said unto his servants: Go ye unto my vineyard, even upon this very choice piece of land, and plant twelve olive-trees; and set watchmen round about them, and build a tower, that one may overlook the land round about, to be a watchman upon the tower, that mine olive-trees may not be broken down when the enemy shall come to spoil and take upon themselves the fruit of my vineyard.

"Now, the servants of the nobleman went and did as their lord commanded them, and planted the olive-trees, and built a hedge round about, and set watchmen, and began to build a tower. And while they were yet laying the foundation thereof, they began to say among themselves: And what need hath my lord of this tower?

"And consulted for a long time, saying among themselves: What need hath my lord of this tower, seeing this is a time of peace? Might not this money be given to the exchangers? For there is no need of these things.

"And while they were at variance one with another they

became very slothful, and they hearkened not unto the commandments of their lord. And the enemy came by night, and broke down
the hedge; and the servants of the nobleman arose and were
affrighted, and fled; and the enemy destroyed their works, and broke
down the olive-trees.

"Now, behold, the nobleman, the lord of the vineyard, called
upon his servants, and said unto them, Why! what is the cause of
this great evil? Ought ye not to have done even as I commanded
you, and—after ye had planted the vineyard, and built the hedge
round about, and set watchmen upon the walls thereof—built the
tower also, and set a watchman upon the tower, and watched for my
vineyard, and not have fallen asleep, lest the enemy should come
upon you?

"And behold, the watchman upon the tower would have seen
the enemy while he was yet afar off; and then ye could have made
ready and kept the enemy from breaking down the hedge thereof,
and saved my vineyard from the hands of the destroyer" (D&C
101:43–54).

Assume, in the world today, that the precious twelve olive trees
are our children and families and that the Lord has placed us on
earth in choice lands and circumstances to live and prepare to
return to him. To protect us, the Lord has constructed a hedge
about us. The hedge separates us from the world, where the enemy
lives. Today's hedge might be the standards of the gospel, set in
place to prepare our youth for all the blessings of the gospel. We are
safe, provided we follow the Lord and receive protection from the
hedge. To warn of coming dangers, a tower, or place of elevation, is
provided where the Lord's watchman can dwell, observe, and warn.
Humble servants are employed to build the tower.

Today's tower is both real and figurative. A temple may be
thought of as a tower. It is a beacon where gospel truths, including

the Atonement, are taught in simplicity and truthfulness. Other elevated views that give us an advantage in seeing and recognizing the enemy include modern-day revelation, living prophets, new scripture, and priesthood authority to perform sacred ordinances. Standing atop the towers are the watchmen.

"The imagery of *watchman* is fitting for those fifteen men who have been called by the Lord as prophets, seers, and revelators, who have been sustained as such by the Church, who have been anointed of the Lord, and who serve as His special witnesses.

"They have been so designated by the Lord in the various dispensations of time. They are found in the Old Testament, the Book of Mormon, and the Doctrine and Covenants, identified as those who are to watch over His Church.

"The term *watch* helps to define their roles which, in part, are: to be attentive to trends, drifts, and conditions within and without the Church; to be vigilant and alert to dangers from the archenemy, Satan; to guard, tend, heed, and warn."[4]

Ezekiel was a watchman. The Lord told him, "Son of man, I have made thee a watchman unto the house of Israel: therefore hear the word at my mouth, and give them warning from me" (Ezekiel 3:17).

"Son of man, speak to the children of thy people, and say unto them, When I bring the sword upon a land, if the people of the land take a man of their coasts, and set him for their watchman: If when he seeth the sword come upon the land, he blow the trumpet, and warn the people;

"Then whosoever heareth the sound of the trumpet, and taketh not warning; if the sword come, and take him away, his blood shall be upon his own head. He heard the sound of the trumpet, and took not warning; his blood shall be upon him. But he that taketh warning shall deliver his soul.

"But if the watchman see the sword come, and blow not the trumpet, and the people be not warned; if the sword come, and take any person from among them, he is taken away in his iniquity; but his blood will I require at the watchman's hand.

"So thou, O son of man, I have set thee a watchman unto the house of Israel; therefore thou shalt hear the word at my mouth, and warn them from me" (Ezekiel 33:2–7).

Despite the challenge of the enemy to destroy the precious olive trees and the fruit of the Lord's vineyard, the Lord's watchmen—the prophets, seers, and revelators—warn and correctly teach and interpret the word of God for all God's children.

PROPHETS WARN AND SPEAK TRUTH

The day the Church was organized in 1830, the Lord told the Prophet Joseph Smith that his calling was to warn the people to give heed to the commandments of God: "Wherefore, meaning the church, thou shalt give heed unto all his words and commandments which he shall give unto you as he receiveth them, walking in all holiness before me; for his word ye shall receive, as if from mine own mouth, in all patience and faith.

"For by doing these things the gates of hell shall not prevail against you; yea, and the Lord God will disperse the powers of darkness from before you, and cause the heavens to shake for your good, and his name's glory" (D&C 21:4–6).

The rebellious want prophets to speak only "smooth" things: "This is a rebellious people, lying children, children that will not hear the law of the Lord: which say to the seers, See not; and to the prophets, Prophesy not unto us right things, speak unto us smooth things, prophesy deceits" (Isaiah 30:9–10).

Things that are "smooth" are agreeable and free from harshness.

But true prophets do not prophesy deceits; they prophesy truths, which the wicked take to be hard (1 Nephi 16:2).

Jacob taught that true prophets speak things that might be hard but that are welcomed by righteous: "O, my beloved brethren, give ear to my words. Remember the greatness of the Holy One of Israel. Do not say that I have spoken hard things against you; for if ye do, ye will revile against the truth; for I have spoken the words of your Maker. I know that the words of truth are hard against all uncleanness; but the righteous fear them not, for they love the truth and are not shaken" (2 Nephi 9:40).

That which is hard is firm, strong, free from weakness or defects, and resistant to pressure. God's prophets will always stand their ground against wickedness. They will always warn us of the enemy. They will always teach us truth. And they will always help us understand the true doctrines of the Atonement of Jesus Christ.

NOTES

1. *Gospel Truth—Discourses and Writings of George Q. Cannon*, comp. Jerreld L. Newquist, 2 vols. in 1 (Salt Lake City: Deseret Book, 1974), 197.

2. Gordon B. Hinckley, *Teachings of Gordon B. Hinckley* (Salt Lake City: Deseret Book, 1997), 28.

3. Boyd K. Packer, "Atonement, Agency, Accountability," *Ensign*, May 1988, 69–70.

4. Lucile C. Tate, *Boyd K. Packer—A Watchman on the Tower* (Salt Lake City: Bookcraft, 1995), vii.

CONCLUSION

The Prophet Jacob said, "For why not speak of the atonement of Christ, and attain to a perfect knowledge of him, as to attain to the knowledge of a resurrection and the world to come?" (Jacob 4:12).

Physical death inevitably awaits all who live, generating perhaps the most universal inquiry of mankind: "If a man die, shall he live again?" (Job 14:14).

The answer to this question is found in the scriptures and revealed doctrines of The Church of Jesus Christ of Latter-day Saints. The necessity of physical death as an absolute condition for all the children of God was clearly explained by Alma as he taught his son Corianton the conditions resulting from the transgression of Adam and Eve in the Garden of Eden.

"Now behold, my son, I will explain this thing unto thee. For behold, after the Lord God sent our first parents forth from the garden of Eden, to till the ground, from whence they were taken—yea, he drew out the man, and he placed at the east end of the garden of Eden, cherubim, and a flaming sword which turned every way, to keep the tree of life—

"Now, we see that the man had become as God, knowing good and evil; and lest he should put forth his hand, and take also of the tree of life, and eat and live forever, the Lord God placed cherubim and the flaming sword, that he should not partake of the fruit—and thus we see, that there was a time granted unto man to repent, yea, a probationary time, a time to repent and serve God.

"For behold, if Adam had put forth his hand immediately, and partaken of the tree of life, he would have lived forever, according to the word of God, having no space for repentance; yea, and also the word of God would have been void, and the great plan of salvation would have been frustrated.

"But behold, it was appointed unto man to die—therefore, as they were cut off from the tree of life they should be cut off from the face of the earth—and man became lost forever, yea, they became fallen man" (Alma 42:2–6).

From the beginning, man was appointed to die. That fact must be understood. So many of life's challenges and concerns would be eliminated if men understood and accepted the universality of death and the promise of the Atonement. President Boyd K. Packer provided this assurance: "If you understand the great plan of happiness and follow it, what goes on in the world will not determine your happiness."[1]

Knowledge of the plan of redemption, or the great plan of happiness, is available to all who sincerely seek truth. Alma testified of the purpose of the plan of redemption:

"Now, if it had not been for the plan of redemption, which was laid from the foundation of the world, there could have been no resurrection of the dead; but there was a plan of redemption laid, which shall bring to pass the resurrection of the dead, of which has been spoken.

"And now behold, if it were possible that our first parents could have gone forth and partaken of the tree of life they would have been forever miserable, having no preparatory state; and thus the plan of redemption would have been frustrated, and the word of God would have been void, taking none effect.

"But behold, it was not so; but it was appointed unto men that they must die; and after death, they must come to judgment, even that same judgment of which we have spoken, which is the end.

"And after God had appointed that these things should come unto man, behold, then he saw that it was expedient that man should know concerning the things whereof he had appointed unto them;

"Therefore he sent angels to converse with them, who caused men to behold of his glory. And they began from that time forth to call on his name; therefore God conversed with men, and made known unto them the plan of redemption, which had been prepared from the foundation of the world; and this he made known unto them according to their faith and repentance and their holy works" (Alma 12:25–30).

The testimony of angels and of prophets is available today just as it was anciently. President Hugh B. Brown declared:

"Sooner or later life's vicissitudes bring each of us to grips with this important subject [the immortality of the soul and man's relationship to Deity], giving us cause to reevaluate our convictions, to reexamine our faith in this essentially spiritual aspect of our religion. Each of us, regardless of color, creed, or nationality, has a rendezvous with the experience that we call death.

"The question of the immortality of the soul is the most persistent, the most universal inquiry of all time."[2]

President Brown further testified of the quest all people have for assurance that life extends beyond the grave:

"The supreme appetite of man is for life—harmonious, eternal life. Nature provides for the complete fulfillment at some time or place of all of the appetites of man. The desire for immortality is the supreme, the eternal, the everlasting desire.

"When I consult my own inner consciousness I find a deep-seated—in fact, an instinctive—feeling of immeasurable oldness, an echo of time immemorial, as well as a feeling of necessary end-lessness. No logical reasoning can dispel these feelings. I did not put these feelings in my inner self; I found them there when I grew old enough to introspect my mind. In spite of recurring doubts and criticisms, there they have remained. If we believe in man's divine origin, we must conclude that mankind has a mission that cannot be encompassed in mortality; that power had a divine purpose that cannot be fully employed or utilized during earth life; that every faculty has a function, even though some are not in evidence in our earthly environment."[3]

I believe we have an eternal mission that does not end with death. I know that the promise of life after death is true and that through the gospel we can perfect our lives by overcoming sin and transgression.

One of the greatest of all incentives for obtaining a testimony of the Atonement is belonging to a family. I am grateful to be a member of a large extended family. My family roots go deep into the soil of the restored gospel, generating within me a sense of heritage and legacy. Despite hardship, my ancestors gave their all to help establish and spread the gospel during the decades since the Restoration. Their suffering and perseverance strengthen my desires to be worthy of gospel blessings.

We face trials and obstacles today similar to those of our

ancestors. Death and the challenges of life prompt us to question life's fairness and to ask, "Why?" Having a personal witness of Jesus Christ and a testimony that he fulfilled the will of the Father in working out the Atonement for all mankind can help us through difficult days of doubt and despair.

Victor Hugo described his hope and anticipation of the marvelous and wonderful life that follows death:

"The nearer I approach the end the plainer I hear around me the immortal symphonies of the world which invites me. It is marvelous yet simple. For half a century I have been writing my thoughts in prose and in verse; history, philosophy, drama, romance, tradition, satire, ode and song; I have tried all. But I feel I have not said the thousandth part of what is in me. When I go down to the grave I can say like many others,—'I have finished my day's work.' But I cannot say, 'I have finished my life's work.' My day's work will begin again the next morning. The tomb is not a blind alley; it is an open thoroughfare. It closes on the twilight, it opens on the dawn. My work is only beginning; my work is hardly above the foundation. I could gladly see it mounting forever. The thirst for the infinite proves infinity."[4]

The gospel of Jesus Christ is true. The Savior wrought the Atonement for our benefit and eternal joy. His resurrection from the tomb is one of the best-attested facts in all history. The Prophet Joseph Smith saw the Son standing on the right hand of the Father, and prophets today continue to receive revelation from Jesus Christ to guide mankind in the ways of truth and righteousness.

I have come to know the truthfulness of these things. It is my hope that this book has assisted you in acquiring your own testimony of these sacred truths.

NOTES

1. Boyd K. Packer, "The Father and the Family," *Ensign*, May 1994, 20.
2. Hugh B. Brown, "Immortality," *Improvement Era*, June 1967, 26.
3. Brown, "Immortality," 27.
4. Brown, "Immortality," 27.

INDEX

13, 151; law of Moses prepared for mission of, 25–27; types and shadows of, 27–29; confirmed law of Moses to the Nephites, 29–30; and the Creation, 35; role of, 38–39; mission of, 53, 60, 69–70; is only means of overcoming the Fall, 55; in Gethsemane, 64–69; testified of the Atonement to the Nephites, 74–75; birth of, 77; sacrifice of, 78; attributes of, 79–81; voluntarily gave his life, 82–83; explained his voluntary offering to the Nephites, 83; voluntarily suffered for us, 83–85; suffered alone, 85–89; was without sin, 89; is our advocate and mediator, 90–92; condescension of, 92–96; made the plan active, 103–6; as Mediator, 116–19; King Benjamin foretold coming of, 133; baptism symbolic of, 143. *See also* Atonement

John the Revelator: on the War in Heaven, 15–16; in Gethsemane, 65

Joseph (husband of Mary), 79

Justice: Atonement satisfies demands of, 73; mercy satisfies demands of, 101, 137, 147; and the Atonement, 109–10; mercy and, 112–16, 116–18

Kirtland Temple, 145

Korihor, 152–54

Law of Moses: and the principle of sacrifice, 21–22, 78, 89; and the Atonement, 25; prepared for Christ's mission, 25–27; types and shadows of, 27–29; and Nephite prophets, 29–33

Lehi: on redemption, 1; on Adam and Eve, 45–47; on false doctrine, 154–55

Letters of repentance, 114–15

Levitical Priesthood. *See* Aaronic Priesthood

Lucifer. *See* Satan

Mankind: role of, 4–5; creation of, 44–47

Marriage, 144–45

Mary (mother of Jesus), 77, 79–80

McConkie, Bruce R.: on the Atonement, 3, 12–13, 18; on sacrifice, 22; on the Passover, 24; on "three pillars of eternity," 37; on the Creation, 41–42; on Adam and Eve, 48–49; on the Fall, 52–53; on Gethsemane, 64–65, 66–67; on Christ's attributes, 80; on Christ as advocate, 90–91; on the condescension of God, 93–94; on covenants, 138–39; on baptism, 139, 144; on "new and everlasting covenant," 144–45

Melchizedek Priesthood, 137, 141

Mercy: satisfies demands of justice, 101, 137, 147; and the Atonement, 109–10; justice and, 112–16, 116–18

Michael, 66. *See also* Adam and Eve

Millet, Robert L., on the condescension of God, 94

Moral agency. *See* Agency

Moroni: on the law of Moses, 27; on the Fall, 53; on little children, 126–27

Moses, law of. *See* Law of Moses

Moses, testifies of the Creation, 42–44

Mount of Transfiguration, 65–66

Nephi: on the Atonement, 7, 156; on the law of Moses, 26–27, 29; on Mary, 79–80; on the condescension of God, 92–93; on covenants, 139; on the lost doctrine of the Atonement, 156–57

Nephites: offered sacrifices, 22; understood the law of Moses, 26–27, 29–33

Nibley, Hugh, on the Atonement, 15

Nicodemus, 143

Oaks, Dallin H., on justice and mercy, 115–16

Obedience, 59, 83

Ordinances, 102, 122, 137–47, 144

Packer, Boyd K.: on justice and mercy, 116–18; on the Atonement, 156–57; on the plan of happiness, 164

Passover, 23–35

Paul: on the law of Moses, 25; on the